Light of Harvest

Amazing Visions a Reality of Open Heaven

Angela Goonewardene

Angela Goonewardene

authorHOUSE®

AuthorHouse™ UK
1663 Liberty Drive
Bloomington, IN 47403 USA
www.authorhouse.co.uk
Phone: 0800.197.4150

Published by AuthorHouse   03/20/2015

ISBN: 978-1-4567-8816-2 (sc)
ISBN: 978-1-4772-3114-2 (e)

Print information available on the last page.

Scripture quotations marked KJV are from the Holy Bible, King James Version (Authorized Version). First published in 1611. Quoted from the KJV Classic Reference Bible, Copyright © 1983 by The Zondervan Corporation.

This book is printed on acid-free paper.

Jesus And Me

"Surely the Lord will do nothing, but he revealeth
His secret unto his servants the prophets."
Amos 3:7

*"Write the vision, and make it plain upon tablets,
that he may run that readeth it. For the vision is yet
for an appointed time, but at the end it shall speak,
and not lie, though it tarry, wait for it, because
it will surely come, it will not tarry."*
Habakkuk 2:2-3

"For God so loved the world, that he gave his only begotten Son, that whosoever believeth in him should not perish, but have everlasting life. For God sent not his Son into the world to condemn the world; but that the world through him might be saved."
John 3:16-17

"There is therefore now no condemnation to them which are in Christ Jesus, who walk not after the flesh, but after the Spirit. For the law of the Spirit of life in Christ Jesus hath made me free from the law of sin and death."
Romans 8:1-2

"Therefore if any man be in Christ, he is a new creation: old things are passed away; behold, all things are become new."
2 Corinthians 5:17

"Now faith is the substance of things hoped for, the evidence of things not seen."
Hebrews 11:1

"Extracts from the Authorized Version of the Bible (The King James Bible), the rights in which are vested in the Crown, are reproduced by permission of the Crown's Patentee, Cambridge University Press".

Dedication

I dedicate this Book to God my Heavenly Father
who loves me,

Jesus Christ my Saviour who died for my sins,

and the Blessed Holy Spirit who empowers

and guides me.

Acknowledgments

I am deeply grateful to the Pastors and Members of the People's Church Assembly of God in Colombo, Sri Lanka, for their encouragement and support in my journey of faith in the Lord Jesus Christ.

I am very thankful to Joyce Cooper, J. Robson and Margaret Gaulton for their willingness to invest their time in providing expert editorial assistance.

I would like to express my deep appreciation to June Ryde, Frank Taylor, Julie Robson and Janet Sinclair for their generous support and prayers during my times of need.

I am also very grateful to my family and friends who upheld me with their continual prayer support over the years of my walk with the Lord and during the publication of this book.

Contents

Forewords

My friend Angela:

I have known Angela Goonewardene for over 30 years. The one thing that impresses me about her is that throughout that period of time Angela's faithfulness to God has been totally consistent and unwavering. Over the last 20 years I have seen her come through various difficult situations, and in spite of it all, her faith in God has become stronger. This has been a great encouragement to me. Angela has always been involved in the world of Biblical literature, which I believe has inspired the vision that arose within her heart, which has now been fulfilled by the grace of God. Her writings of these visions in the "Light of the Harvest" booklet have been inspiring and real. I pray that God will meet your need as you discover the words that God has revealed to Angela in this new publication.

Fredrica Perera,
Elim Pentecostal Church, London

****

God has given us special gifts and abilities. Based on teaching in God's Word, we are shown how to recognise those gifts and how to develop and use them in God's service.

Angela has done just that with the "LIGHT OF THE HARVEST" book. I believe this book is a key ingredient in the believer's daily life and gives us an understanding of God's plan and purpose for our life and journey in this world. This book is also a great witnessing tool and a conversation starter; I would recommend everybody to have a copy of this handy when you are out and about. They say that a book or anything written reflects the author, and this is true as to the "LIGHT OF THE HARVEST", as it reflects the Creator through Angela's life, her dedication to the cause of Christ and personal testimony of what God is doing in her life.

Please support Angela in the furtherance of getting the gospel across to a dying world by purchasing this effective tool. Love God with all your heart and support your neighbour as yourself!

Joash Perera
London, England

Introduction to the Light of the Harvest

Dear Friends,

The "Light of the Harvest" book came about when the Lord spoke to me from His Word in **2 Kings 4:7** "Go, sell the oil, and pay thy debt."

As I have been serving the Lord for many years I thought I was doing what the Lord wanted me to do. Then in 2005 the Lord gave me a vision of a book; the name was **"Light of the Harvest"**. A page in the booklet was opened and I saw the **face of Jesus,** and **facing that page were many families and people**, and there were many more blank pages in the book. I had no clue at that time. Within a couple of months the Lord showed me in a dream to start the **next page** of the same book, with **"Jesus and me"** and I started writing my personal testimony.

As I was thinking of the name "Light of the Harvest" the Lord revealed to me that **Jesus was the Light** and the **People were the Harvest.**

Many times the Lord had spoken to me to **(Habakkuk 2:2-3)** "Write the vision, and make it plain upon tablets, that he may run that readeth it. For the vision is yet for an appointed time, but at the end it shall speak, and not lie: though it tarry, wait for it, because it will surely come, it will not tarry".

In 2006 the Lord showed me in another dream that the booklet was finished, and to start printing it. This was very hard for me to do as I had no money. I contacted many publishers and printers, but as there was no money I delayed. Then the Lord spoke to me in the early hours of the morning when I woke up to read my Bible **"Write the vision upon tablets"** a clear message once again, and to **establish what I have to establish.** I thank God that in a miraculous way and in obedience to Him I have been able to print the book.

I felt I must share this with you all, as the Lord gave me another message to *"launch out into the deep, and let down your nets for a draught".* **(Luke 5:4).** Many people are interested in visions and dreams and testimonies sometimes when they make a decision for Christ. My friends and believers who have read my original booklet have encouraged me and have informed me that it is good and presentable to bless loved ones and friends so that they too can have a closer relationship with the Lord. My prayer is that the Lord will richly bless you as you read this book, which is an **upgraded version.**

Miss Angela Goonewardene

****

Part 1

JESUS AND ME

PERSONAL TESTIMONY
GOD OPENED MY EYES OF UNDERSTANDING

I was born into a Roman Catholic family. We grew up in a strict Catholic background. I firmly believed that this was the right way. However, my older brother had accepted Jesus as his personal Saviour. He was an ardent reader and a member of a couple of libraries. He used to read various types of books—novels, philosophy, science, psychology etc. One day he brought a Bible into our home and that was the first time we had set eyes on a Holy Bible. When he started reading it, I observed him and was rather amazed that he hadn't finished reading it. Then I asked him "Brother, when are you going to finish reading that Bible? Usually you finish a book in a few days, but this book has taken so long. Haven't you finished it?" He replied, "This is the first and last book I will never stop reading." I was surprised at his answer. Quite often he spoke to me on the book of Proverbs in the Bible, knowing my interest in proverbs, but my mother always advised me never to listen to him. He spoke to me of accepting Jesus Christ as my personal Saviour, referring to the book of John chapter 3, about how to be born again. I always told him that I only pray to Jesus and I have been doing it since my childhood. I couldn't understand what he was trying to tell me, so I used to question him and even get irritated with him.

Two months elapsed and my brother had been praying for me. One day my cousin and I saw him reading the Bible and we sat on either side of him asking him to explain the Bible to us. He explained from John chapter 3 saying, "Unless one is born again, he *CANNOT **SEE*** the Kingdom of God, and unless he is born of water and the Spirit, he *CANNOT **ENTER*** the kingdom of God." This verse spoke deep into our hearts, and to his amazement, we both accepted the Lord Jesus Christ as our personal Saviour. Very soon we were baptized in water by immersion. After a couple of months, I attended a 'Christian Convention' and heard how to receive the Holy Spirit. I joined the youth group that day and prayed with them. That same night before I went to bed I knelt at my bedside and prayed for just a few minutes, as I did not know how to pray. I got into bed still thanking and praising the Lord when suddenly I burst into stammering lips, and an unknown tongue, I knew I had received the Holy Spirit. I was bubbling with unspeakable joy.

One important thing my brother taught me was to read the Bible every day and spend a little time with the Lord in prayer. This I did and the Lord enabled me to grow, gradually making me a mature Christian. I could not keep this joy within myself but started sharing and witnessing to my two sisters and friends. After that, I gave up my secular job and started serving the Lord at the International Correspondence Institute (Bible Correspondence) run by the Assemblies of God in Sri Lanka. As a result, the Lord used me to win many souls into His Kingdom. Later the Lord brought me in a miraculous way to work in England at the International Correspondence Bible Study. God has very graciously enabled me to study His Word in depth through the ICI Bible Study courses which are designed and arranged very systematically at the ICI UNIVERSITY in USA. I praise and thank God for His Mighty Hand upon my life, His rich blessings and the marvellous way He leads and guides me every step of the way. **Proverbs 11:30** "The fruit of the righteous is a tree of life; and he that winneth souls is wise." **Daniel 12:3** "And they that be wise shall shine as the brightness of the firmament; and they that turn many to righteousness as the stars for ever and ever."

Angela Goonewardene

****

TESTIMONIALS

I have known Angela Goonewardene as a mighty woman of God for many years, who is deeply passionate in winning souls for Jesus at any cost. She is someone who is unique and has dedicated her whole life for the work of the Lord. She is also an anointed woman of God, used powerfully to change lives of others. To her obedience to God, she has written this book and I am sure everyone who reads this book will surely be blessed mightily.

Mihitha Dehideniya,
High Barnet, England

****

During the 16 years that I have known Angela Goonewardene she has consistently demonstrated holiness and victorious living through her strong faith. Her main purpose and heart is to see people come to know Jesus and acknowledge Him as their personal Saviour. She is publishing this book as an evangelism tool in obedience to His Word. You will be truly inspired as you read about the visions that have been revealed to her.

Julie Robson,
Kent—England

ANGELA'S JOURNEY OF REACHING PEOPLE FOR JESUS

By Dr Astrid Aiyadurai

Angela and I have been close friends and prayer partners for almost thirty-five years. I have seen that her love for Christ and her zeal for evangelism have never waned, but have grown stronger over the years. In Sri Lanka, while residing together with her at the Marian Hostel, and attending the People's Church Assembly of God, Colombo, we would go witnessing door to door inviting people to come to church or attend special meetings. We would also meet regularly in the prayer room in church and pray together for the evangelization of Sri Lanka and for the whole world.

In order to pursue her passion for evangelism and in obedience to God's call upon her life, Angela resigned her secular job and began working in full-time ministry with the International Correspondence Institute. In her ministry with ICI she was conscientious and hard-working and she would constantly explore new opportunities to reach the unsaved with the good news of the gospel of Jesus Christ in Sri Lanka and abroad. Through her faithful efforts, many unbelievers came to faith in Jesus Christ and began growing in their faith with the aid of the evangelistic and discipleship tools of ICI.

Then Angela decided to step out in faith, extend her borders and pursue her dream to reach the world for Jesus Christ. As the doors of opportunity have opened Angela has relentlessly continued to pursue her passion for evangelism. First she began her ministry overseas with the ICI Bible Study office in the UK, then at Kensington Temple (Evangelism Department) London and Premier Christian Radio London and later in various churches in London.

The "Light of the Harvest" records Angela's love relationship with her Saviour and Lord Jesus Christ, her pilgrimage of faith and her passion for evangelism. I believe this book will be a powerful evangelistic tool that will be used in the lives of many around the world, to draw them into an ongoing relationship with Jesus Christ.

****

THE REDEEMED OF THE LORD

A VIVID DREAM the Lord gave me on the 24th of June 1977.

Habakkuk 2:2-3 "Write the vision, and make it plain upon tablets, that he may run that readeth it. For the vision is yet for an appointed time, but at the end it shall speak, and not lie; though it tarry, wait for it; because it will surely come, it will not tarry."

I call it a Night Vision: I saw that I was carried still in my blue night-gown and found myself in a very large place. There was great darkness there and I saw many silver pillars, which were about six feet tall and shone like stars. I was standing near one pillar and I saw these pillars reaching as far as my eyes could see. It was a very vast place and the pillars were not countable. There was a place which was not ready, as the foundation of the building was to be laid. There was a tall white lady who was showing me the building and the person who was in the building was asleep so I was afraid to go in there. I stood near another silver pillar and stretched out my hand saying, I haven't been to this side, I haven't been to that side, and I had in mind to go to the nearby places. I was also looking out at the pillars far away as far as my eyes could see and they were smaller than the silver pillars close by because they were beyond where my eyes could see. However, I had in mind to go as far as I could go. I learnt that Silver can mean Redeemed, the pillars around six feet tall were redeemed people, redeemed by the Blood of the Lamb.

A part of this night vision was fulfilled when I commenced work at the International Correspondence Institute (Bible Study) in April 1978 and started preparing the ground to spread the Word through the Bible Correspondence in Sri Lanka. We started sending out Bible Correspondence on the 25th of January 1979. The work expanded very rapidly and we had about six to seven full-time staff members. We organised ICI Rallies and had the privilege of meeting hundreds of students. At the end of the first course, "The Great Questions of Life", we directed them to the nearest Evangelical church in their local area.

****

THE HALLELUJAH VISION
OF FIVE HOURS
Preparing the Bride for the soon coming Bridegroom

This is the five hour vision that the Lord gave me on the **25th of August 1981.** I was very ill on my bed with a very high fever and thought I was dying. I was feeling a numbness within me and my feet felt like fire. During that time, I had been working at the International Correspondence Institute in Sri Lanka for three and a half years. I really enjoyed working through the Evangelism courses we used to witness, in the ICI Ministry. Many students studied the Word of God, about 2500 accepted Christ as their Saviour and Lord. As I was very sick, I felt that my work for the Lord was over and I was going to be with Jesus very soon.

At midnight on the 24th August 1981 I heard a beautiful Hallelujah song sung by 'hosts of Angels', one which I had never heard before. It continued with adult voices for a few minutes, followed by young voices which sounded like cherubims and seraphims. As it was going on for a very long time, I too sang from time to time with the angelic voices, softly, as I was very ill. I saw young children coming towards me. Some came in groups, some in twos and threes and some were alone. They all came towards me. Some were smiling, and others had questioning faces. I saw thousands of them right throughout the Hallelujah chorus which was still going on. Then I saw many young people in groups of twos and threes and single kneeling and praying: seated and praying and standing and praying; after that they were dressed in 'white robes' and entered into a very large hall, taking their seats. One side of the hall was getting filled, and the rest of the hall had empty chairs.

After that I was taken to see many churches big and small, and in every church there was a small group of people dressed in white robes and made ready. Then I heard loud music with drums and cymbals and bells etc., and saw a very long procession of beautiful people dressed in shining robes. On their heads they had something glittering like crowns with precious stones, and they were marching on a street of transparent gold. At this time I did not hear the Hallelujah song but very loud music like drums and cymbals. When I heard it I said to myself, "This sounds like Pentecostal music". While passing by everyone looked at me with smiling faces. The procession took a very long time and there were thousands, I couldn't count. After that the loud music stopped and once again I heard the same Hallelujah song. Finally, I saw a double bed. I noticed the bed stand was shining and on my right side I saw a person dressed in light blue. He was about six feet tall, lying on the bed. His eyes were wide open and He looked a Sri Lankan of Eastern colour. The most vivid thing I noticed in Him was that He was FULL OF LIFE which really amazed me as here I was dying. Then the Hallelujah song stopped and I got up. I looked at the time and it was 5.00 a.m. sharp on the 25th of August 1981 and the vision was over.

When I woke up in the morning I was fully aware that I had seen a vision as I was up and had had no sleep throughout the five hours. The vision was very **vivid.** I still remember it. I prayed and asked the Lord for the interpretation of the vision. It took one full year for me to understand many things in the vision and the interpretation.

The one who was lying on the right side of the double bed was the Lord Jesus Christ. I understood that He took my place, He died to set me free from my sins and sicknesses, He gave me eternal life. He gave me victory over death, hell, and the grave. He represented the Sri Lankans and because He lives, we also live. He gave me new life and used me as an instrument in His Mighty Hands. As He died for the whole world, so He died for the Sri Lankans as well. He gave me a new lease of life to continue His marvellous work.

The young people whom I saw smiling and coming towards me were students to whom I have witnessed through the International Bible Correspondence Ministry in Sri Lanka. As Christ was on my right side the students were smiling with Him. I believe they saw Christ in me. I was only His instrument used as His witness to the students. Jesus said "You are my witnesses". The empty chairs on the one side of the large hall showed me that my work was not over as the Lord had a plan for me to complete the work He had given me.

In obedience to Him I continued the work at ICI (Bible Correspondence) for twelve and a half years and I was tested and tried from time to time. The vision was given to me lest I fall short of my commitment. Every time I was tested the vision came to my mind—it was a challenge to me, I could foresee the future through the vision. The Lord used me to witness to over a hundred thousand students in Sri Lanka and at least seventy five thousand students had accepted Jesus Christ as their personal Saviour through the Bible correspondence in Sri Lanka during a period of twelve and a half years.

The double bed symbolises marriage. I believe the Lord is preparing the bride for the soon coming Bridegroom. Jesus had Life in Him even as His Word says, **John 11:25** "I am the resurrection, and the life: he that believeth in me, though he were dead, Yet shall he live."

The procession I saw were the students to whom I had witnessed and who have accepted Christ as their Saviour and Lord through the Bible correspondence. The many churches I saw in the vision were the churches where the students attended. There were small groups of people dressed in white and ready in every church I saw in the vision.

The people entering the large hall who were dressed in white were the people whom the Lord was preparing as His bride, the students to whom I had been witnessing.

1 Thessalonians 4:16-18 "For the Lord himself shall descend from heaven with a shout, with the voice of the archangel and with the trump of God: and the dead in Christ shall rise first: Then we which are alive and remain shall be caught up together with them in the clouds, to meet the Lord in the air: and so shall we ever be with the Lord. Wherefore comfort one another with these words." **I Corinthians 15:51-54** "Behold, I show you a mystery; we shall not all sleep, but we shall all be changed, in a moment, in the twinkling of an eye, at the last trump:

for the trumpet shall sound, and the dead shall be raised incorruptible, and we shall be changed. For this corruptible must put on incorruption, and this mortal must put on immortality. So when this corruptible shall have put on incorruption, and this mortal shall have put on immortality, then shall be brought to pass the saying that is written, Death is swallowed up in victory." **Colossians 3:4** "When Christ, who is our life, shall appear, then shall ye also appear with Him in glory." **1 John 3:2b** "When He shall appear, we shall be like Him; for we shall see him as He is."

God is not a respecter of persons. If we belong to the family of God He can use anyone who is yielded to Him and is desiring to serve Him as His instrument, to prepare the bride for the soon coming Bridegroom. **Zechariah 4:6b** "Not by might, nor by power, but by my spirit, saith the Lord of hosts."

A DREAM: A BRIDAL OUTFIT

During the time I was working at International Correspondence Institute—Bible Correspondence in Sri Lanka I had a dream that I was wearing a beautiful white bridal garment with gold embroidered work on it. This bridal outfit had more gold embroidery on it than white; I could hardly see the white garment. There were a few people whom I saw in white garments in bridal outfits. One of my friends with whom I was working at that time was with me as well. She too had a beautiful white bridal garment just like mine, but she had less gold embroidered work on it. I was also wearing a long white bridal veil which had gold embroidered work. However, I knew that my work on the veil was not fully complete. When I woke up in the morning I prayed and asked the Lord for the meaning. These words were given to me from within; I believe it is from the Holy Spirit. **Tested with fire and come through as gold**. I also knew that my work was not complete as my veil was not fully completed.

A few years later I left the International Bible Correspondence Institute as I knew I had to move on. However, I believed I had more work to do for the Lord and I continued His work at my Church at Impetus Ministries Trust, which was another ministry of our Church, until I came to England and joined the International Correspondence Institute BIBLE STUDY here in the United Kingdom. While at work in this office I had the privilege of studying the Bible in depth and was able to follow diploma and degree courses in

Christian Ministry and Christian Doctrine through the systematically designed Bible study courses arranged by the ICI University in USA. I thank the Lord I was able to continue the work of the Lord in various ways using my time and my talents for His glory as a result of studying His word.

MEETING JESUS ON A HEAVENLY
FLIGHT OF STAIRS

A Beautiful Dream on the 25th of August 1982

A dream that I can never forget. It was so vivid that I still remember it very well. I was thinking of Jesus and the HALLELUJAH vision He had given me on the 25th August 1981, especially the person who was at the end of the vision who was full of life.

The Dream: There were many rows of flights of stairs. I saw that my mum took me to a flight of stairs and she was not sure which flight of stairs I should climb. When I saw the first one I said it was my brother's flight of stairs, so I got on to the second one—it was extremely high but I managed to climb half-way through and very quickly I was right up the stairs with just two more steps to climb when I saw from a distance the tall figure of the beautiful Saviour Jesus Christ the Son of God in a long white robe coming down very quickly to meet me. When He came up to me I only saw His white robe and His hands which looked as if He was holding a lantern, but the light was on His hands. Praise God! I could not believe that Jesus my Saviour came down to meet me when I got to those heavenly stairs. I had only two steps more to climb and the place was fully lit up. When I woke up in the morning I had forgotten the dream. However, that same day when I returned from work and was climbing stairs to go into my room I believe the Holy Spirit reminded me, and the whole dream came back to my mind and it was very vivid.

Jesus revealed to me in a dream that He was the last person whom I saw in the HALLELUJAH vision, as I had a question and was very keen to know the last person in the HALLELUJAH vision. It took one year for me to know the full meaning of the previous Hallelujah vision. Praise God! He communicates with us, His children, when we have questions. This dream made me so happy to know that unworthy as I am, Jesus the Son of God came down to meet me as I had only two more steps to climb and the place was fully lit up. I believe the light is the presence of the Lord Jesus Christ.

A DREAM GIVEN BY THE LORD IN OBEDIENCE TO READING THE NEW TESTAMENT—1982

I loved reading the Old Testament more than the New Testament. However, from time to time when I got a full day's holiday, I took time to read the whole Book of Revelation in one day, at least two or three times a year. When I read the Old Testament I never read it in order, just opened and read it. Then the Lord in a dream showed me to read the New Testament and He showed me that the Old Testament is ancient and I saw the book of the Old Testament in very small print and it looked as if it was very far away. I saw the New Testament in large print very close to me. When I woke up in the morning I knew that the Old Testament was something of the past and is a type of the New Testament which is of the present and is now relevant to this time. So I made it a point to read the New Testament and started reading the whole New Testament from the very beginning of Matthew to the book of Revelation. When I finished reading it, the Lord gave me a beautiful dream.

The Dream: I saw that I was taken to a place which looked like a very large estate with many, many trees. They were extremely tall; I couldn't even imagine reaching out to them. I passed all these trees, looking at them in amazement. When I came to the end of it there was my tree, tall and lovely, and the name HEPHZIBAH was written on it, and next to my tree there was another small tree shooting up beautifully. Then I woke up. I was so happy when I thought of the beautiful place where I was in that dream, and I was thinking of the interpretation. I believe even as we read and meditate on the Word of God, we have a two way conversation with Him. He speaks to me in dreams and visions to confirm His Word.

I remembered the word HEPHZIBAH in the Bible in Isaiah and I quickly turned to Isaiah and found it in **Chapter 62 Vs. 4-5** "Thou shalt no more be termed Forsaken; neither shall thy land any more be termed Desolate: but thou shalt be called Hephzibah, and thy land Beulah: for the Lord delighteth in thee, and thy land shall be married." I learned that Hephzibah means **"that the Lord delighteth in you".** Praise God, since then I started reading the whole New Testament in order, and now from 1989 I started reading the whole Bible in a year from my "Daily Devotional Bible" This is awesome! I delight in reading His Word and I know God is delighted with me as He has shown me very recently—in 2004 when I took another Christian book to read He spoke to me in a dream, to **read the Scriptures**, although I did read the Bible every day, yet He has shown me I am to spend more time reading the Word than other books. He is so real I know He sticks close to me, even closer than a brother, and directs me every step of the way. I love my God for being so involved with every minute detail in my life. He is my Abba Father.

Psalm 1:2-3 "But his delight is in the law of the Lord; and in his law doth he meditate day and night. And he shall be like a tree planted by the rivers of water, that bringeth forth his fruit in his season; his leaf also shall not wither; and whatsoever he doeth shall prosper."

****

Part 2

JESUS AND ME

HIGHLIGHTS OF VISIONS AND DREAMS

A LONGING DESIRE TO SEE THE FACE OF JESUS

This dream was in 1983. I had a longing desire to see Jesus face to face when I had a dream. First I saw my face and then the face of Jesus was appearing in front of me. Again I saw my face, and then the face of Jesus appeared in front of me. This happened twice. I did not have to look at a mirror to see my face; my face was extremely beautiful and resembled His face. The Holy Spirit revealed to me that Christ's image is formed in me. This is how I saw Jesus in me face-to-face. Some day when we go to heaven our Heavenly Father will see Christ in us, the hope of glory. The blood of Jesus has paid it all. **John 17:24** "Father, I will that they also, whom thou hast given me, be with me where I am; that they may behold my glory, which thou hast given me; for thou lovedst me before the foundation of the world." **Ephesians 1:4** "According as he hath chosen us in him before the foundation of the world, that we should be holy and without blame before him in love". **1 Peter 1:19-20** "But with the precious blood of Christ, as of a lamb without blemish and without spot. Who verily was foreordained before the foundation of the world, but was manifest in these last times for you."

A DREAM IN 1983

I was working at the International Correspondence (Bible) Institute; there were two people present in the office at that time, one colleague was seated at the other end of the room far away I could have hardly seen. Suddenly I felt a light breeze from where I was seated in the room and I told my close colleague who was working with me, "There is a breeze outside: I want to see". I got up and walked towards the door at the entrance of the office, suddenly I was taken up, and up, and up, I felt very light in my body and I saw myself as if I was inside a shiny-white balloon. Finally I ended up in the air. I did not see anyone there but there was a lot of light in that place, then I woke up. I believe it was a meeting in the air. **Matthew 25:13** "Watch, therefore; for ye know neither the day nor the hour in which the Son of man commeth."

ANOTHER DREAM IN 1983

I had spent quite some time in prayer for worldwide revival. In answer to prayer the Lord gave me a dream that I was in a very large stadium with many white people lifting up their hands and praising the Lord. The place was filled with bright lights, and packed to capacity. I had no clue at that time where it was, I only knew it was worldwide. This dream came to pass when I came to the United Kingdom: I was able to attend many Prayer Conferences at Birmingham, Mission to London evangelism meetings at Earls Court, and many other meetings and Conferences in England and London.

4th **March 1998**—I was praying to get a job in a Christian Institution. Early this morning in a dream in answer to prayer, I saw the letters "Congratulations! Administration". They were written in big bold letters and shown to me in my room. I was also shown a lovely blue dress folded and kept on my dressing table which was ready for me to wear and some notes of money as well. A couple of days later I got my first job in a Christian Institute. I thank the Lord the dream came to pass; God is so involved in our day to day life. **Acts 2:17-18** "And it shall come to pass in the last days, saith God, I will pour out of my Spirit upon all flesh: and your sons and your daughters shall prophesy, and your young men shall see visions, and your old men shall dream dreams: And on my servants and on my handmaidens I will pour out in those days of my Spirit; and they shall prophesy:"

6ᵗʰ June 1998—This was a time I was attending Hills Christian Life Church in London now known as HILLSONG London; I was very much involved in evangelism in various ways, and distributing tracts and Premier Christian Radio programme schedules as well. I woke up early in the morning with these words, **LEADER, MOSES, 8000**. I believe the Lord gave me these words to encourage me due to my enthusiasm in evangelism and the Lord was going to bless me with 8000 souls as a result of evangelism, I presume I will see them in heaven. God does nothing without revealing His secrets to His servants the prophets.

13ᵗʰ November 1998—A dream from the Lord. I saw a big gold instrument handed over to me. The one who was carrying it had two instruments; one was given to me and the word **Sceptre** came from within me. Praise God! **Sceptre** (meaning a staff carried by a sovereign as symbol of authority—sovereignty or royal authority). I believe this ministry, in God's eyes, is very significant although in the sight of people it can be very insignificant. God is good! I have been praying at one time to keep me insignificant in the sight of people. I know for sure that the Lord is working with me, He said He will never leave us nor forsake us. He is preparing us to be kings and priests for Him. **Revelation 1:6** "And hath made us kings and priests unto God and His Father; to Him be glory and dominion for ever and ever. Amen".

JESUS WAS STANDING AT THE DOOR
I saw Jesus face to face, Jesus said
"Thank you, I am coming soon!"

25th June 2001—A Vivid Dream: Prayer is a two-way conversation with the Lord. Very often when I pray the Lord does speak to me through dreams, visions and from His Word to confirm what I have been praying. It is His way of communicating with me. I praise God for my Lord and Saviour who is so close to me when I really need Him.

This dream the Lord gave me when I started praying for the back-slidden people in the Church and for my close loved ones. I saw that Jesus was coming to our house and the sky was very red. I was in a room with many people and they were all asleep. I was walking up and down in the room expecting Jesus to come at any time, when suddenly I looked up at the sky, the clouds were red and in a twinkling of an eye JESUS came down from the sky and He was standing at the entrance of our house. I quickly woke up a lady saying `auntie, auntie, get up, Jesus has come to our house`, and the lady woke up. I saw JESUS face to face from where I was standing. To separate Jesus and me there was only a golden grille between us. (Jesus' face was sad, the crucified suffering Christ who died for us and has paid such a great price.) Jesus looked at me but it was as if He was looking beyond and he said "THANK YOU". He also said "I AM COMING SOON". Then I woke up. I was amazed at the dream because I saw Jesus face to face. Only a golden grille separated both of us. This means JESUS is at the

DOOR, HE IS COMING SOON. I firmly believe He wants to wake up all those who are spiritually asleep. He was encouraging me to pray for my loved ones and for the church family, Jesus has a compassionate heart for you and me. God has revealed Himself through His Son Jesus who shed His precious blood for us on the Cross of Calvary. He wants to see everyone saved and ready for His soon return. Our passion should be to pray for all our families to be reconciled to God, I praise God for this dream. God loves us with an everlasting love. We all must respond to His love.

A VERY VIVID DREAM IN 2001

This was a Wednesday when I used to fast and pray at the Intercessory Prayer at the Ladies' meetings in the church. I prayed for revival for our local community. The very next day the Lord gave me a dream, where I was standing at the pulpit in the church with many others and there were many gathered around the stage, all dressed in white. The people were white people. Everybody was singing the song **"Cover Me"**.

"Cover me, Cover me, extend the borders of your mantle over me, for you are my nearest kinsman. Cover me, cover me, cover me." (this refers to the Book of Ruth) **Ruth 3:9**

It was amazing that nobody had to teach the words as everybody knew the song. There was a man representing this community who is a Christian whom I knew, singing the same song. Praise God! I believe the Lord communicates to me in this way that my prayer is answered and that He is preparing the Church and this community for the soon coming of the Christ. The people were white people. Jesus represents the white people even as He represents the Eastern and African people. (Boaz and Ruth are a type of Christ and the Church).

20ᵗʰ December 2003—A week before Christmas I made an extra effort to do two weekly bulletins for Christmas for Elim Church, although I was going on leave. On the front of the bulletin was the song **"Joy to the world, the Lord is come"**. I wanted to do my best and on Friday the 19th with joy I displayed them in the church as usual. Early Saturday morning I had a dream that there was a beautiful **gold bulletin** on the table in the foyer. This was the end of the year. The Lord has shown me that my works have been tested with fire and have come through as gold. Praise God! He has honoured the jobs I have been doing in the church and also the bulletins for His glory. The Lord is good, He is concerned in every little job we do for Him and He has encouraged me to continue to be faithful in His work. I'm glad I'm not working alone as I'm always aware that the Lord is working with me according to His Word. **Mark 16:20** "And they went forth, and preached everywhere, the Lord working with them, and confirming the word with signs following. Amen."

19th March 2004—The Lord gave me a beautiful dream early this morning in response to what I have been listening to and reading about Father God and His love for His children. On the 18th night I started reading the book on the **Father's love letter** to His children, before I went to sleep, and I believe this is how the Father communicates with me sometimes in dreams and visions.

In the Dream: I saw many little children in a large hall and at the end of the hall on the right side there was a table set and Jesus was sitting at the table. He looked young, with hair and a beard as well. There were only children seated at His table and on the floor; I did not see any adults. I walked into the hall and saw all these children close to Jesus. They were seated in the presence of Jesus and had little baked cakes in their hands. There were some children far away in the hall as well. Then I saw myself entering the hall and I looked right in and saw Jesus at the table and I thought, "Why must I stay here at the back?" I walked right into the hall and came and stood at the right side of Jesus with my hand round Him, probably on the arm of his chair; Jesus turned around and offered me a piece of bread from His hand, even as He had given the kids little cakes. I broke off a small piece, from Jesus' hand but I did not feel any flesh when I took the bread. I believe it is because God is a Spirit and Jesus has a glorious body. This relates to the little jobs I have been doing for kids' programmes in the Church. I praise God for revealing Himself to me in this way. **Mark 10:15-16** "Verily I say to you, whosoever shall not receive the kingdom of God as a little child, he shall not enter therein. And he took them up in his arms, put his hands upon them, and blessed them."

If you have never accepted Jesus Christ as your Personal Saviour and Lord and wish to invite Jesus into your heart say this prayer with all your heart now:

Heavenly Father, I believe You sent Your only Son Jesus Christ to die on the cross of Calvary for our sins. Lord Jesus, I acknowledge I am a sinner, I repent of all my sins; forgive me, wash me and cleanse me with Your blood. I believe You rose from the dead. I receive You as my Saviour and Lord, come into my heart, save my soul, I give You my life. Fill me with Your Holy Spirit. Lead and guide me to live for You all the days of my life. Amen.

Luke 15:10 "In the same way, I tell you, there is rejoicing in the presence of the angels of God over one sinner who repents."

John 17:26 "And I have declared unto them thy name, and will declare it: that the love wherewith thou hast loved me may be in them, and I in them".

Heb.1: 3 "Who being the brightness of his glory, and the express image of his person, and upholding all things by the word of his power, when he had by himself purged our sins, sat down on the right hand of the Majesty on high;"

****

PART 3

JESUS AND ME

"Draw near to God, and he will draw near to you".
James 4:8
The closer we get to God the more He will reveal Himself to us.

Dreams, visions and encouraging words, given to me by the Holy Spirit.

12ᵗʰ June 1998—Ministering Angels
This was an early morning dream. I saw a huge angel standing in the air who was looking down at me. I was looking up at the angel and I felt very little in his sight as he was so huge. I believe he is the angel whom the Lord has sent to protect me and fight my battles. He has won the victory for me, therefore he was smiling at me. Jesus' blood has won the victory for me as I have accepted Jesus Christ as my personal Saviour and Lord.

Many times the Lord has shown me ministering angels when I was alone or needed some kind of protection. There was a time when my friend with whom I was residing had gone abroad on holiday and the Lord revealed to me in a dream before I woke up, that there were angels walking up and down the stairs in long white robes, and I was very confident that I was not alone.

Another time when I was concerned and even afraid as my friend was on holiday abroad and had parked her the car on the side entrance of our house, I prayed for protection and the Lord gave me a dream that I was singing the song "Your angels attend me, You shelter me round like the Cedars of Lebanon when I lay me down", and in the dream I saw policemen guarding the house. The Lord reminded me that he has sent his angels to protect the house. **Psalm 91:11** "for He shall give his angels charge over thee, to keep thee in all thy ways."

Again on another occasion I wanted to go abroad on holiday and I was concerned during that time whether I should travel as I had no money. I was praying about it and the Lord revealed to me in a dream—a tall angel dressed in a long white robe brought down my travel suitcase from the attic from where it was stored, and there was clean money in the case. I still remember the angel in the long white robe walking very quickly down my stairway. I was amazed at this dream when I woke up that night. It took some time for me to get my travel suitcase down from the attic. The Lord provided the money through my church and friends who generously gave me the money for my travel abroad.

26th December 1998—A CLEAN RECORD—In a dream I saw a pure white book with gold all around the pages of the book; it looked like a diary, very clean pure white. I was just turning the pages all around and found it pure and white, no marks anywhere, only gold on the edge of all the pages and all around. Praise God. Jesus has won the victory for me by His blood and made me white as snow. **1 John 1:7** "But if we walk in the light, as he is in the light, we have fellowship one with another, and the blood of Jesus Christ his Son cleanseth us from all sin."

24th July 2002—I woke up in the morning with the words, **"Worship the Lord with all your heart for God wants to bless you".** I believe this is the Holy Spirit speaking to me, I did take it seriously. I started spending more time with the Lord and He started blessing me in various ways. The Lord's desire is to see that the plans He has laid out in our lives are fulfilled when we seek to follow Him diligently. He knows our weaknesses and He wants to help us by speaking to us, so that we will be strengthened in the faith when we take delight in Him and His word. It's all to do with **Jesus and me**. He wants to see His image formed in us. Even as His word says in **Psalm 37:4** "Delight thyself in the Lord; and he shall give thee the desires of thine heart."

14th May 2004—A Glimpse of My Father God
I was reading the devotional book, The Father's Love Letter. Early this morning in a dream I saw Father God's face, He had a soft smile, hair golden, very strong arms, powerful and beautiful. I only had a glimpse of Him, but it gives me great joy every time I think of Him. As it is written in the book I have been reading, God is the perfect Father I have been looking for all these years. I felt the Father's presence watching over me and this gave me immense security. What a great big wonderful Father we all have, only if we can recognize and acknowledge Him as our Father or Abba Father. I'm looking forward to seeing Him one day when the Lord takes me to heaven as He has promised us everlasting life.

John 14:8-9 "Philip saith unto him, Lord show us the Father and it sufficeth us. Jesus saith unto him, Have I been such a long time with you, and yet hast thou not known me, Philip? He that hath seen me hath seen the Father; and how sayest thou then, Show us the Father?" **In Hebrews 1:2-3** you will read that Jesus is the brightness of His glory and express image of the Father.

18th June 2004—"All Israel will be saved." These words came from within me late last night in answer to prayer, as I pray for the Peace of Jerusalem every day. When I accepted the Lord as my personal Saviour and started reading the Bible, I came across **Psalm 122:6** "Pray for the peace of Jerusalem; they shall prosper who love thee." The Lord even revealed to me the many precious gifts He has for us, as a result of praying for the peace in Jerusalem. The Lord has many surprises for the little things we have been doing on this earth in obedience to His word. I thank the Holy Spirit for giving me a desire to pray for the peace of Jerusalem every day.

19th October 2004—A message from His Word in answer to prayer regarding my work in the Lord.

"See that you complete the work you have received in the Lord" **Col. 4:17.**

During this time I was going through some trials and this was a word given to me by the Holy Spirit to strengthen me and to continue the work of the Lord. The Lord revealed to me that He is my comforter, helper and provider and He will bless me and meet all my needs, including finances. I then prayed and asked the Holy Spirit to keep me faithful in fulfilling His plan and purpose in my life and to give me His grace to serve Him even better as long as I live. God is faithful, He keeps to His promises.

11ᵗʰ May 2005—Early this morning I received these words from the Holy Spirit, **"I Will Build My Church."** I believe Jesus is confirming His Word when we pray for the Church. The spreading of the Good News of the gospel of the Kingdom will continue from victory to victory until Jesus comes back in glory. **Matthew 16:18b** Jesus said; "I will build my church; and the gates of hell shall not prevail against it". When we pray for the Church He will lead and guide us by His Holy Spirit, and show us how to be a witness and a blessing to our loved ones, friends and many acquaintances who are blindly stepping into a lost eternity without Salvation. God does not want anyone to perish. His word says that we are His witnesses. Jesus paid the price with His own precious blood on the cross of Calvary, and He wants to bless everyone who accepts Him with eternal life**. John chapter 17** is one of the best prayers Jesus ever prayed for the Church and for many who will accept Him and follow Him wholeheartedly.

12ᵗʰ May 2005—I had a dream that my bed was filled with heavenly dew, it was like a white veil, and I took an edge of my blanket and squeezed it and took a handful of water from it, and **someone said, the Bridegroom is coming soon.** I believe Jesus is coming very soon! Praise the Lord! When I woke up I said "Jesus, prepare me for Your soon return". Dreams and visions are a great encouragement given to us by the Holy Spirit as we seek to love the Lord with all our heart, all our soul, all our mind, and all our strength. God will reveal Himself to us when we abide in His word and apply His word into our lives and situations. God wants us to meditate on His word day and night. When we read the Bible we can get rooted and grounded in the Word. His word says to put on the whole armour of God if we want to fight the enemy who accuses us of sin and condemnation as we continue to follow the Lord faithfully.

26th June 2005—In this early morning dream I saw that my mum and sister were on a very high mountain and I walked up and joined them and I said, "Mummy, it's snowing" and I was holding my hands out and white snow was falling on my palms and Mum said, "Look up the higher mountain, there is so much snow fallen there". We were very far from there, although we were on a very high mountain. Praise God! I believe Jesus is giving us revival.

10th August 2005—A word from the Lord early this morning. **"Be confident, seek the Lord".** I received these words because I was anxious about Jesus' coming. These words encouraged me even more to seek the Lord, trust Him, love Jesus and take Him at His word. God gave up His only begotten Son to gain our love. We should never doubt God's unfailing love towards us. When we continue to follow our Lord and Saviour with confidence He will continue to bless us with all spiritual blessings. His one desire is to draw us more closer to Him. According to **Ephesians 1:3** God has blessed us with all spiritual blessings in heavenly places in Christ.

8th September 2005—Another dream similar to the one I had seen on the 26th of June, 2005. I was on a very high mountain with many green trees. It was beautiful, the sun was shining. I was with my mum and I told her, "Mummy, see there is snow on the top of the trees". I praise God for this beautiful dream. I believe the sun was the presence of the Lord and the snow was like the dew from heaven. Mummy and I were in a higher mountain than in the previous dream I had seen. Praise the Lord, God has many surprises for us when we all get to heaven.

8th October 2005—"Be confident, seek the Lord." This is the second time I received these words before I woke up this morning; very encouraging because I was so anxious and looking forward for His coming. The Lord wants me to be confident and I believe He is assuring me that I can trust Him. God wants to demonstrate His love towards us by speaking to us in this way, and confirms His promise for a second time. I just love the Lord, for His mercy endures forever.

11th October 2005—In a vision this morning I saw a very large place full of light with children smiling and clapping their hands. As far as my eyes could see they were all children in that large place. Heaven will be filled with children. It can be the children who were lost in the Pakistan earthquake, or God is raising up a new generation of children to praise Him. **Psalm 127:3** "Lo, children are an heritage from the Lord; and the fruit of the womb is his reward".

2nd November 2005—I woke up this morning seeing a dream that my hair was black and very long, almost down to my ankles. I combed it, with my hair on my lap; I was seated in a bus with a close relative. I said "It's the first time I have had my hair so long". This is in answer to prayer, as I had been praying that the Lord will forgive all those who have wronged me, including my loved ones, friends and all work colleagues. The Lord wants us to forgive people who have wronged us and not hold any grudge against anyone, even as He forgave all our sins by shedding His precious blood on the cross of Calvary, and did not hold us guilty of our sins. Jesus is Holy and we have to live holy lives if we want to spend eternity with the Lord. Long hair can mean the anointing from the Lord. **John 12:3** "Then took Mary a pound of ointment of spikenard, very costly, and anointed the feet of Jesus, and wiped his feet with her hair: and the house was filled with the odour of the ointment".

19th November 2005

1. **Give your best to God and He will give His best to you.**
2. **From the beginning of this year to the end of next year there will be revival.**
3. **I was in the spirit in the last days of time.**

All these words were given to me by the Holy Spirit between 3.30 a.m. and 4.00 a.m. The Lord wants us to invest our time and talent in the Lord's work, so that He can give His best to us. Prayer is a vital part in our daily lives, to hear the voice of God. When we give ear to Him as He speaks to us and obey His voice, He will take care of our needs. He is an all knowing, all powerful and a merciful God, who wants to bless us with good gifts even before we could ask or think, in appreciation of His love to us. We see the hunger in the hearts of people as they respond, when they hear the Good News. I understand that revival is taking place even now, as we pray and tell others about the Lord's goodness and love towards them.

People are desperate to know the love of God as they live in this period of God's grace and mercy. God has commanded us to go and preach the gospel to all the world. When we lift Jesus high, He will draw all men unto Him. The Lord's desire and plan for all mankind is to pour out His Spirit upon all flesh. When the body of Christ is filled with the Holy Spirit great and mighty signs and wonders can take place in these last days of time. **Acts 2:17-18** "And it shall come to pass in the last days, saith God, I will pour out of my Spirit upon all flesh; and your sons and your daughters shall prophesy, and your young men shall see visions, and your old men shall dream dreams; and on my servants and on my handmaidens I will pour out in those days of my Spirit, and they shall prophesy."

22nd November 2005—Words given to me from the Lord early this morning. **Put on the whole armour of God. Get excited at His coming.** We must meditate on His word day and night, as the enemy the devil comes like a roaring lion and tries to devour especially the Christians and their families. It's always good to apply and claim God's word and be covered by His precious blood so that the enemy won't have an opportunity to touch the Christians and their families. I believe Jesus is coming very soon even as He said, this is why He wants us to get excited at His return. It gives me joy to hear such beautiful words from the Holy Spirit in the early hours of the morning, especially when I take time to read God's word and spend time with Him.

9th December 2005—A word from the Lord when I woke up this morning. **Returning of the Jews and the Christians**. I have seen and heard through Christian TV and radio that many Jewish people are turning to Jesus, and Christians and Jews are joining hands in worship and praising God together in answer to prayer for revival. The Lord is awakening the hearts of Christians to love the Jewish people and to pray for the peace of Jerusalem as He has promised to prosper those who love them.

7th January 2006—**We are so close to the glory of God.** Words from the Lord in the early hours of the morning. I was so delighted to receive these precious words, and to know how the Lord speaks in a still small voice into our hearts, especially when we continue to read God's word, and learn to be in His presence by the help of the Holy Spirit in our daily walk with Jesus. The more we pursue to know the Lord the more He will help us by His Spirit to get more close to Him. **1 John 3:2b** "When he shall appear, we shall be like him; for we shall see him as he is".

30th January 2006—**Born of His Spirit, washed in His blood.** Wonderful words I received early this morning before I woke up. God reveals himself to us through His word. We already have the victory in Christ Jesus. Praise God for the assurance given to us, that we are redeemed by the Blood of the Lamb—Jesus Christ. **Heb.9:22b** "And without shedding of blood is no remission." There is no forgiveness of sins unless through the blood of Jesus. **Ephesians 1:7** "In whom we have redemption through his blood, the forgiveness of sins, according to the riches of his grace."

31ˢᵗ January 2006—Words given to me by the Holy Spirit as I woke up this morning.

1. **God is love and His love is everlasting.**
2. **Covenant keeping God He is.**

The Lord revealed to me that He is a covenant keeping God through a message I received, it is permanent. Father God wants to lavish His love on us. God has made a covenant with Noah and with Abraham, and Jesus has made a covenant with us which is the New Covenant, when He shed His precious blood and died on the cross of Calvary for our sins. These awesome words give me the desire to love the Lord even more. What a privilege it is to hear the voice of the Lord speak deep into my heart. **Luke 17:21** "Neither shall ye say, Lo here! or lo there! for, behold, the kingdom of God is within you".

6ᵗʰ February 2006—I have placed watchman on your walls. 6.19 a.m. A word from the Lord in answer to prayer as I had fasted and prayed for the peace in Jerusalem. I presume this word is for all the Church to pray for the peace in Jerusalem. In my opinion, we the Church can hasten the coming of the Lord as we pray and seek God's face. We have been placed as watchmen on the walls of Jerusalem; this is a command to all believers. Only the Lord can bring peace on the earth. Jesus the Prince of peace has the answer. He has even promised to prosper those who pray for the peace of Jerusalem. According to **Psalm 122:6** "Pray for the peace in Jerusalem; they shall prosper who love thee."

9th February 2006—Words given to me very early this morning by the Holy Spirit.

1. **The Churches, all the churches were flowing with milk and honey.**
2. **The Lord will bless you with new hope, a fresh anointing oil that will flow through you to touch the hearts of people.**

Jesus is the Head of the Body of Christ, we the Church are anointed by the Lord to spread the Good News of the Kingdom to all the world. This is a command by the Lord to tell people about Him. In obedience to His word and with the help of the Holy Spirit we can be a witness to many; the Lord in return will bless His people, and turn many to righteousness. I'm thankful to the Lord for enabling me to be a witness to my friends, loved ones and acquaintances, whom I meet in various ways in my day to day life. But deep within me I feel an urgency of the great commission Jesus has given us, to go into all the world and preach the gospel.

God desire is to establish all believers, of the church of Jesus Christ, to fulfill His plan and purposes. God's heart yearns to restore all men unto Him. God is ever-loving, always forgiving, full of compassion; what incredible love Father God has for us, if we can only grasp His abounding love to respond to the Father's heart. How much more will He be able to accomplish through us, to win the lost from a dying world. Jesus said "I will build my church and the gates of hell shall not prevail against it."

14th **February 2006**—A word from the Lord before I woke up this morning. **You will be led and guided by the Holy Spirit.** This word gives me great confidence in the Holy Spirit. Whenever the Lord wakes me up in the early hours of the morning, I spend time reading the Bible. When we delight in the Lord, and walk in His anointing, He will demonstrate His love by assuring us of His abiding presence always and that He leads and guides us through the power of His Holy Spirit. **2 Corinthians 13:14** "The grace of the Lord Jesus Christ, and the love of God, and the communion of the Holy Spirit be with you all. Amen."

15th **February 2006**—This was an early morning dream. I saw myself praying with two other ladies in a circle with one accord. I prayed saying "Lord I come into your presence through the **blood of Jesus**" and there was light in His presence before I woke up. The Lord has shown me many times to come into His presence through the **Blood of Jesus.** Jesus' blood is pure Royal Blood that flowed from Calvary's cross for our sins and sicknesses. Jesus was pure, holy and sinless before God and man. His work on the cross was perfect, a complete finished work. God manifests His amazing love for the whole Body of Christ in this way. God is an ever-loving Father who gave His only begotten Son to die for us. Jesus redeemed us through His precious blood.

8th **March 2006**—A pure white envelope with the beautiful name of Jesus Christ written in gold letters was placed on the second step of the stairs of my home, as if it had come through the letter box of my house. Praise God! I believe this was like an invitation from the Lord or a thank you card as I had given some finances for the GOD TV Channel. I believe God wants us to help spread the Good News of the Kingdom in this way, as the God TV Channel reaches out to over 200 nations.

This is an opportunity for us to reach out to people, where we cannot go, but Satellite TV can reach to the uttermost parts of the world. What a privilege this is for believers who want to reach out to the lost into the uttermost parts of the world, and be a blessing and a witness to many who do not know the Lord. Thousands and thousands of people come to know the Lord through TV and radio and the Internet. When we hear and see the testimonies on Christian TV and radio it gives us joy to be a part of God's work. How much more God is pleased with us when He sees Jesus being lifted up on the earth, He is the only one who can draw all men unto Him. **John 14:6** "Jesus saith unto him, I am the way, the truth, and the life; no man cometh unto the Father but by me."

9ᵗʰ March 2006—These words were given to me early this morning. **No more crying, no more pain**. Amazing words of love! I thank the Lord for these comforting words given to me by the Holy Spirit. Especially when we face anxieties in many ways the Lord speaks comforting words. He knows and understands all that's going on deep down in our hearts, Father God's love is everlasting and is compassionate, He loves us very deeply. Jesus displayed God's compassionate heart by His actions in healing and delivering the multitudes that followed him daily during his public ministry on this earth. In **Revelation 21:4** we read that God will wipe away all tears from their eyes, and there will be no more crying and no more pain. What a great big wonderful God we serve.

25th March 2006—God is going to keep you from all evil. I was glad to hear these words from the Holy Spirit early this morning. God makes Himself real to us by the power of His Holy Spirit who lives and works in our lives on a daily basis. In the Lord's Prayer we pray that the Lord keep us from all evil. This is confirmation from the Lord as a result of having a two-way conversation with Him. When I asked the Lord to fill me with His Holy Spirit, I was blessed with unknown tongues, my experience with the infilling of the Holy Spirit was joy unspeakable, this was evidence that I had received the Holy Spirit and was filled with power from on high. When we speak in unknown tongues we speak mysteries with God.

I thank the Lord for the beautiful love relationship I have with Him through the power of His Holy Spirit. I praise Him for all that He has done for me, and for all that He is going to do, in keeping me from all evil. Jesus' name is powerful, the evil one trembles when we mention the name of the Jesus. At the name of Jesus every knee shall bow and every tongue shall confess that Jesus Christ is Lord. According to **Psalm 91** in the Bible "Because thou hast made the Lord which is my refuge, even the most high thy habitation, there shall no evil befall thee, neither shall any plague come near thy dwelling." We also read in the book of **I John 4:4** "Ye are of God, little children, and have overcome them, because greater is he that is in you than he that is in the world."

2nd July 2006—Blessings forever! I was delighted to hear encouraging words from the Lord early this morning. When we pray and read the Bible, He will speak to us through His word. The Holy Spirit brings us to a place of intimacy with Christ, we are reconciled to God because of the great sacrifice Jesus has done for us by shedding His precious blood for us. When God sees us He sees Christ in us, because of the faith we have in Christ, and the blood of Jesus cleanses us from all sin. What a privilege to hear and know the blessings from the Lord whispered deep down into our hearts by the Holy Spirit. The Lord manifests His love and abounding grace towards us in this way. I'm glad I can proclaim the blessings of God, and walk in His favour all the days of my life.

2 Corinthians 5:21 "For He made Him who knew no sin to be sin for us, that we might become the righteousness of God in Him." **Psalm 23:6** "Surely goodness and mercy shall follow me all the days of my life; and I will dwell in the house of the Lord forever."

15th August 2006—Israel—during the Lebanon War.
I had been praying for the peace in Jerusalem during the war in Lebanon. Many Christians were praying for the Peace of Jerusalem, for victory over the war and the salvation of Jews and Gentiles when many Arabs and Jews were accepting the Lord during that troubled time in their temporary shelters. I was not sure why Israel could not claim victory over the war in Lebanon, because it is the Lord who fights the battles for Israel, as He has promised in His word. I had been questioning the Lord as I had been praying for the peace in Jerusalem; then

I received these words from the Holy Spirit early this morning at 3.00 a.m. which was like a prophetic word in answer to my question and prayer. **This is a year, for nearly 2000 years of staggering years, I the Lord will do a new thing. Do not look upon the outward appearance, but on the inward heart**.

I believe the Lord gave me the assurance that from the year 2000 things have changed and the Lord is speaking to people in various ways and many are turning their hearts to the Lord by the power of the Holy Spirit in this 21st century, therefore I should not worry or look to the outward appearance of what the media says regarding the war between Israel and Lebanon, but look to the inward heart of the people whom the Lord is changing and preparing by His Holy Spirit in these last days, as Jesus is coming very soon.

What an awesome powerful God we serve in this day and age. **ICorinthians 15:51-56.** "Behold I show you a mystery: We shall not all sleep, but we shall all be changed, in a moment, in the twinkling of an eye, at the last trump; for the trumpet shall sound, and the dead shall be raised incorruptible, and we shall be changed. For this corruptible must put on incorruption, and this mortal must put on immortality. So, when this corruptible shall put on incorruption, and this mortal shall put on immortality, then shall be brought to pass the saying that is written, death is swallowed up in victory. O death, where is thy sting? O grave, where is thy victory? The sting of death is sin; and the strength of sin is the law, but thanks be to God who giveth us the victory through our Lord Jesus Christ."

19ᵗʰ September 2006—I woke up with these words this morning. I will take care of your need and I will make thy name great. Genesis 12:1-2 "Now the Lord had said unto Abram, Get thee out of thy country, and from thy kindred, and from thy father's house, unto a land that I will show thee: And I will make of thee a great nation, and I will bless thee, and make thy name great; and thou shalt be a blessing". Praise God for His faithfulness to Abraham and all his descendants. The Lord has given us these promises and He is fulfilling them in various ways as we continue to walk in His ways. I pray every day to the Lord to make me a blessing to someone each day and to help me use my time and talents for His glory.

Due to the innumerable ways of opportunity we now have, with all the modern equipment and advanced technology which is a great contribution, we are able to spread the Good News of the Kingdom to all the world as a witness before the end comes. The Lord has given us the privilege of being a blessing to many around us, for God's glory in this eleventh hour. This may be one of the reasons the Lord said to His disciples that greater things we will do when He goes to the Father. However, we have confidence that with the help of the Holy Spirit we can do all things to spread the Gospel of the Kingdom. Jesus Christ paid the ultimate price for us by shedding His precious, sinless blood on the Cross of Calvary, because of His unfailing love for us.

God's desire is to see man restored back to Him. He does not want to see anyone perish. Hell was created for the devil and his angels who rebelled against God, not for human beings. Therefore, even as the Lord has commanded us, our passion should be to pray for our unsaved loved ones and witness to those who don't know the Lord that they may come to a knowledge of the true and living God. Prayer is powerful; it can bring conviction of sin and true repentance in the hearts and lives of people so that they will turn to God and have a close relationship with Him. **John 3:16-17** "For God so loved the world, that he gave his only begotten Son, that whosoever believeth in him should not perish, but have everlasting life. For God sent not his Son into the world to condemn the world; but that the world through him might be saved."

22ⁿᵈ September 2006—Words given to me early this morning. **I want to be in the first-fruits with Jesus! I'm longing to be with Jesus.** (Today is the feast of Trumpets.) Whenever the Lord wakes me up in the night or in the early hours of the morning, I take the opportunity to read His Word. When our Heavenly Father looks down at us, He doesn't see our sin, but Christ in us the hope of glory. God's grace and favour is on our lives. We must believe and pray to the Holy Spirit that our relationship with Jesus will be true and faithful, not lukewarm, but a strong love as we look forward for the Lord's return; God's heart yearns to see Christ's image formed in us.

I Corinthians 15:22-23 "For as in Adam all die, even so in Christ shall all be made alive; But every man in his own order: Christ the first fruits; afterward they that are Christ's at his coming." **I Thessalonians 5:17** "Pray without ceasing". It reminds us to watch and pray as Jesus has commanded us to do. Jesus said He is coming for a pure bride, even the bride of Christ. As we are in Christ, old things have passed away, all things are made new.

25ᵗʰ September 2006—You are not here by chance or accident but by Divine appointment. **God has a plan for you and a purpose for your life.** I woke up at 4.30 this morning with these amazing words given to me by the Holy Spirit. God has great plans for us, He reveals His plans when we seek Him diligently, continue to follow Him and be a blessing as we share with others the good news of Jesus Christ and His finished work on the cross of Calvary for our sins. The Lord is faithful, He keeps to His promises, I have full confidence in Him, as I have been praying to the Lord to use my time and talents for His glory, and to accomplish His plan and purpose in my life. **Psalm 139:17-18** "His thoughts towards us are countless as the sand on the seashore."

25ᵗʰ April 2007—Year of gladness, joy unspeakable. I woke up with these beautiful words from the Holy Spirit very early this morning. God knows how to bless us with unspeakable joy when we put our trust in Him and continue to glorify His name. He will make Himself known to us in a greater way. The Lord is worthy of our praise. When the Lord speaks to us we must proclaim it, receive it in faith, believe and act upon it, in doing so He can bless us even more.

9ᵗʰ May 2007—I saw myself singing in a dream, "I praise you Lord because you heard me. I praise you Lord for giving me victory". This song I had composed from Psalm 118:21-25. This is a victory song. When we go through problems and difficulties God gives us a song to sing and rejoice in Him. In doing so we can have victory over all problems as the Lord takes control of every situation and reveals to us His righteousness, peace and the joy in the Holy Ghost. The more we spend time in the presence of the Lord, we are assured that we will receive even songs in the night in answers to prayer and win the victory through our Saviour Jesus Christ. **Zephaniah 3:17** "He will rejoice over thee with joy; he will rest in his love, he will joy over thee with singing."

3rd **July 2007**—I was praying in tongues, as the Spirit gave me utterance, when I saw a vision of many children singing, dressed in white with blue ties, and Jesus was in the midst of them; they were smiling as they sang. There was so much light in that place, I believe it was the presence of the Lord, which was awesome. I believe heaven will be filled with children. The Lord is speaking to us to be like little children, when we come to Him. **Luke 18:16-17** "But Jesus called them unto him, and said, 'Permit little children to come unto me, and forbid them not; for of such is the kingdom of God. Verily I say unto you, whosoever shall not receive the kingdom of God like a little child shall in no way enter it' ".

14th **August 2007**—I woke up very early this morning with a word from the Holy Spirit, **The best is yet to come.** This is something I was looking forward to receiving from the Lord, the more I begin to proclaim these words, the more He will show in the realm of the Spirit what God wants to establish in my life. According to **Jeremiah 31:3,** God loves us with an everlasting love. We must proclaim His favour over our lives. I thank God for being so mindful of us; this is a result of having a two-way conversation with the Lord. The more we read and meditate on His Word (the Holy Bible), the more we talk to Him, we will hear His still small voice speaking to us. Nothing is impossible with God.

21st August 2007—This morning as I was praying in the Spirit, I felt the presence of the Lord and **a beautiful gold pendant was given to me. It had the word Bible, on top of it, with colourful precious stones around it.** The Holy Spirit has revealed twice to me in dreams to read the Scriptures, this enabled me to read and meditate on His word even more. I presume God has many surprise treasures stored up in heaven for us when we spend time praying and reading the Bible. What privileges God has given us when we co-operate with the Holy Spirit, listen to His voice and respond in obedience to Him as He reveals His love gifts to us. The book of Psalms does encourage believers to praise and thank the Lord in every circumstance; King David was constantly speaking to God for deliverance as he went through good times and tough times. According to God's word we should pray without ceasing, and meditate on His word day and night. Effective prayer of a righteous person is powerful. In Psalm 141:2 we read, "Let my prayer be set forth before thee as incense; and the lifting up of my hands, as the evening sacrifice."

25th August 2007—The words I received from the Holy Spirit when I woke up in the early hours of the morning to read my Bible: **My crown is awaiting me in heaven.** The words were so encouraging that I wrote them down immediately. When we continue to abide in His love and ask the Lord to reveal Himself to us He hears us. He is faithful to make himself real to us as we listen to His still small voice speaking to us by the power of His Holy Spirit. God's amazing love towards us is unconditional, His desire is to lavish His love on us. The great sacrifice of Jesus made it available for us to have access to God through His blood that was shed on the Cross of Calvary.

We are privileged to be called the children of God, we belong to the Body of Christ, Jesus is the King of kings and the Lord of lords. The Holy Spirit is preparing the Church, the Bride of Christ, for the soon coming of Jesus; He is first coming for His Bride, as we earnestly seek Him and long for His appearing, He will be faithful to keep to His word, God's love and unmerited favour rests upon the Body of Christ. **I Peter 5:4** "When the Chief Shepherd shall appear, ye shall receive a crown of glory that fadeth not away." There are other crowns, like the crown of life, the crown of righteousness. **2 Timothy 4:8** "Henceforth there is laid up for me a crown of righteousness, which the Lord, the righteous judge, shall give me at that day; and not to me only, but unto all them also that love his appearing."

3rd September 2007—Words given to me early this morning by the Lord. **Total image of my favour**. I also saw a figure of the Lord dressed in white robes which covered me totally. I believe it's the presence of the Lord, and this reminds me of the song, "A wonderful Saviour is Jesus my Lord" (Chorus)—"He hideth my soul in the cleft of the rock, That shadows a dry thirsty land, He hideth my life in the depths of His love, And covers me there with His hand."

God's unmerited grace and favour rests on us. We are saved by grace, God has enabled us to sit together in heavenly places in Christ Jesus. When we believe and apply His word into our hearts we can be assured that we are His children.

19th October 2007—Revival—I'm going to see it happen. From the time I accepted Jesus Christ as my personal Saviour and had a close relationship with the Lord, I began to understand about revival. From that time on I had been praying and asking the Lord to bring about a true Holy Ghost revival. I even prayed to see it happen. I have seen revival happen in some Churches but not on a big scale. I continued praying very much for a world-wide revival. I thank the Lord that in answer to prayer, the Lord enabled me to see many revivals take place in churches and Christian organizations in the nations through Christian TV. We are privileged daily to see hearts lives changed in many people young and old accepting the Lord Jesus Christ. Advanced technology has made it possible to reach out to people in the uttermost parts of the world.

As a result, thousands of hearts are open to hear the word of God and have opportunities to acknowledge Jesus Christ as their Lord and Saviour; I see and hear more testimonies of people's lives changed and delivered now than ever before in this day and age through advanced technology. Praise God for the awesome ways God has blessed mankind to come to a knowledge of Him in these last days of revival.

An encounter with Jesus is the best decision one could ever make if they want to spend eternity with God. One must remember this privilege of everlasting life with the Lord is for ever and for ever. God's unconditional love and compassion is manifested in His Son Jesus Christ through His death and resurrection and by the power of the Holy Spirit.

21st October 2007—These comforting words were given to me early this morning by the Holy Spirit when I woke up to read my Bible. God is awesome!

1. **The Lord covers you with His love (1.45 a.m.)**
2. **He makes you a happy organised believer.**
3. **The Lord loves you and cares for you.**

Every morning when I wake up, I pray and ask the Lord to take control and help me organise the day. With His help I have been able to accomplish all I had planned to do and even more, which makes me happy and more organised. This shows that the Lord is working with us as He has promised. He loves to help us even in little things. Jesus is my Best Friend; I can go to Him at any time, night or day, because He has promised never to leave us nor forsake us. We should always claim the promises of God and apply them deep down in our hearts if we want to continue in His love and favour.

15th November 2007—My people, My people, it shall be well with you. These words were so encouraging when the Lord woke me up to read His Word very early this morning. God desires us to read His Word day and night. Many times the Lord has shown me to spend time reading His word. When we delight in Him, He will speak to us in a still small voice by His Holy Spirit.

In another dream I was under a shower. I had a shower in the morning and again another shower in the evening and I saw that my hair was very long, down to my knees. I believe this is a result of reading the Word of God night and day. We must pray and ask the Holy Spirit to reveal His Word, He will surely help us understand and apply it to our lives. He has promised to lead us into all truth. **John 15: 3-4** "Now ye are clean through the word which I have spoken unto you. Abide in me, and I in you. As the branch cannot bear fruit of itself, except it abide in the vine; no more can ye, except ye abide in me." **Joshua 1:8.** "This book of the law shall not depart out of thy mouth; but thou shalt meditate therein day and night, that thou mayest observe to do according to all that is written therein; for then thou shalt make thy way prosperous, and then thou shalt have good success."

25th November 2007—Once again I thank God for the wonderful words I received before I woke up this morning.

1. **The Joy of the Lord is my strength.**
2. **You must thank God for the talents that He has for you.**

The Lord loves to bless us with His joy. The joy that we can earn is to be in His presence and enjoy the Love of God in prayer and worship, singing songs and making melody in our hearts to Him. He also wants us to thank Him for the talents He has given us and use them for His glory and honour and praise. God has blessed everyone with talents. We are responsible for how we can use them for His glory. We read in **Matthew 25:16** "Then he that had received the five talents went and traded with the same, and made them other five talents."

2nd December 2007—The Lord reminded me of these precious words early this morning before I woke up. **God the Father, God the Son, God the Holy Spirit—these Three are One.** There are many who do not believe that the Father, Son and the Holy Spirit are One. There are others who say that it is not mentioned in the Bible. In **I John 5:7-8** we read "For there are three that bear record in heaven, the Father, the Word, and the Holy Ghost: and these three are one." "And there are three that bear witness in earth, the Spirit and the water, and the blood; and these three agree in one." Jesus' great commission to His disciples in **Matthew 28:19** "Go ye, therefore, and teach all nations, baptising them in the name of the Father, and of the Son, and of the Holy Spirit". The Scripture has also proved in many verses in the Bible that the Father and the Son are One.

20th April 2008—In a dream early this morning I saw myself wearing a pure white prayer shawl with tassels on the ends. A prayer shawl is like a gift from the Lord, I believe this is a Prayer Ministry which the Lord has given me as I continue to read His Word and intercede in prayer for many requests the Holy Spirit leads and guides me to pray for every day; for example, the body of Christ—the Church, unsaved loved ones, friends, for those in authority so that we may live a peaceful life, sick people and vulnerable people and many more.

The greatest intercessory prayer was prayed by Jesus to our Heavenly Father in the chapter of John 17:1-26. This is a model prayer for us to learn and know the love of Jesus. If you take time to read John 17, you will notice that Jesus prayed for Himself, for His disciples and He prayed for all Christians in the Body of Christ. Jesus' compassionate heart towards us is abounding in mercy. **John 17:20-22** "Neither pray I for these alone, but for them also who shall believe on me through their word; That they all may be one, as thou, Father art in me, and I in thee, that they also may be one in us; that the world may believe that thou has sent me. And the glory which thou gavest me I have given them, that they may be one, even as we are one."

6ᵗʰ May 2008—I had a dream of a banqueting hall with a table and chairs around; the significant thing I noticed was a beautiful **GOLD CROWN** placed on the table. I have been praying for all my family and loved ones to get saved. Recently, when I started thanking the Lord for their salvation, the Lord gave me this dream of the banqueting table, and the beautiful gold crown. I believe the Lord is preparing my loved ones for His coming in answer to prayer. In a previous dream the Lord gave me a word that my crown is awaiting me in heaven.

18ᵗʰ May 2008—Heaven and earth are full of Thy glory. I was reading my Bible when I received these words into my spirit. The Lord's one desire is to see not only heaven being filled with His glory but the earth as well. When we the saints of Jesus Christ all begin to worship and praise the Lord day and night with one accord, how much more will He be pleased to bless us extravagantly with every spiritual blessing and keep us in perfect harmony with God and man. In the Lord's Prayer we read "Thy Kingdom come, Thy will be done, on earth as it is in heaven."

10th July 2008—I woke up in the early hours of the morning to read my Bible, when the Lord gave me these words, **10,000 churches will be filled with 20,000.** The revival fires are burning all around the world due to the healing outpouring that's happening in Lakeland, Florida, and in many other countries as well. Many unsaved people are being swept into the Kingdom of God in the thousands daily, just by listening to Christian radio, watching Christian television and the Internet, with wonderful programmes of Youth Rallies, Christian Conferences and various speakers from many churches boldly speaking God's word into the hearts and lives of people, where we see change and hear wonderful testimonies of God faithfully fulfilling His word with signs and wonders as the gospel of the Kingdom is preached with power and authority in these end time revivals that are taking place all over the world. As a result there are many churches filled with people being equipped and prepared for the soon coming of our Lord and Saviour Jesus Christ.

16th August 2008—Something greater than a revival is going to take place. These words came from within me by the Holy Spirit, after I had spent time with the Lord in the early hours of the morning. Jesus said, to go into all the world and preach the gospel to every creature. It is a command from the Lord; when we obey the Lord in doing so, He will surely bring about a great awakening, a Holy Ghost revival in these last days to the nations as promised in his word. I believe the Church of Jesus Christ will be a witness and a blessing to all the world and the Bride of Christ will be made ready for the soon coming Bridegroom. Jesus said in His word: **Matthew 24:14** "And this gospel of the kingdom shall be preached in all the world for a witness unto all the nations; and then shall the end come."

7th September 2008—FEAST OF TRUMPETS

Words given to me early this morning. **Today is the First Day of the Final Year, get your trumpets out.** I don't understand why the Lord gave me this word. I believe the Lord wants us to prepare ourselves for the soon coming of the Lord. This word can even be a warning for the Church to prepare for the days ahead, for this can be the beginning of the end. **Joel 2:1** "Blow the trumpet in Zion, and sound an alarm in my holy mountain. Let the inhabitants of the land tremble; for the day of the Lord cometh, for it is near at hand."

10th October 2008—And Jesus on the stairway saw me and blessed me. Wonderful words given to me early this morning by the Holy Spirit just before I woke up. I could visualise Jesus standing on the stairway and blessing me. When we delight in Him and His Word, and long for Jesus, and His presence, He will surely bless us. He is faithful to give us victory over everything we say and do, when we seek Him with all our hearts. God loved us with an everlasting love so that He gave His only begotten Son to redeem us from sin and death. Because of Jesus' death on the cross we were made whole. God is not a respecter of persons. Anyone who will repent and turn from their sin and accept Jesus Christ as their personal Saviour will be born of God and will receive eternal life. It is a free gift from God.

12ᵗʰ October 2008—Early this morning I had a dream that my sister and I were in a very big church, and a friend who was seated next to me was sad and needed prayer. The church was packed with people praying, the preacher was praying as well. In front of the Church right in the middle there was a big lampstand and a fire was burning bright on the lampstand. The glory and presence of the Lord was sensed. I was laying hands on the friend next to me, my sister was stretching out her hands towards the front and we were all praying. This was my sister who had taken water baptism recently. I praise God! The lampstand burning bright was the awesome glory and presence of the Lord. God inhabits the praises of His people.

25ᵗʰ October 2008—Victory in Jesus' Name. Awesome words given by the Holy Spirit before I woke up this morning in answer to prayer. This is a reminder that when we pray and seek the Lord He gives us victory in His powerful Name. Only in Jesus can we receive the victory over any situation we face in our day-to-day life. The Lord always surprises us with powerful words of love when we pray and listen to His still small voice speaking to our hearts so clearly.

16ᵗʰ January 2009—All these words were given to me by the Holy Spirit early this morning, when I woke up to read my Bible. **People all over the world will gather round Jerusalem, Gold for the Jewish people—Victory.** God's plan must be fulfilled in Jerusalem as He has promised.

Man cannot change what God has already ordained for Jerusalem and the Jewish people. This is why we have been commanded to pray for the peace in Jerusalem, so that we too can receive His blessings and security. According to His Word, it is only through Jerusalem that the Lord is going to bless all the nations. The Lord has said in **Genesis 12:3b,** ". . . and in thee shall all families of the earth be blessed." Also **Psalm 121:4,** "Behold, He who keeps Israel shall neither slumber nor sleep."

3ʳᵈ May 2009—Words given to me early this morning before I woke up. **Financial blessing and prosperity**. I have been praying for financial blessings and the Lord has spoken to me on several occasions that He was going to bless me. There are times when we may have to persevere in prayer to receive His blessings, and at other times we have only to speak the word and receive, as His Word says "Believe that you receive them and you shall have them." His timing is the best; He knows the perfect timing for us. I thank Him for His faithfulness. When God gives a promise He keeps to it. I take the Lord at His word. We have only to trust Him and see the promises given to us from His Word being fulfilled.

31ˢᵗ May 2009—I was praying to the Lord for His help as I was getting ready to print this book. I was determined to upgrade this book as the Lord wanted me to do. I was anxious to establish what the Lord wants me to establish with regard to His work. These were the words the Lord gave me before I woke up this morning. **With the Lord all things are possible!** I praise God for the confirmation given to me from His Word to print and publish this book.

29th June 2009—I had a dream before I woke up this morning that I was in the church and there were many people in the church dressed in white. I joined a small group with about five or six ladies; we held hands to pray and I heard a voice saying **"The Power House is settled".** I believe these words were given to us by the Holy Spirit. White garments are pure and clean in the Lord's sight. The Lord is encouraging the Church to join hands and pray together. He wants us to know that there is power in prayer when we pray together—**Matthew 18:19-20.** "Again I say to you that if two of you shall agree on earth touching anything that they shall ask, it shall be done for them by My Father, who is in heaven. For where two or three are gathered together in My name, there am I in the midst of them."

23rd July 2009—Words given to me early this morning by the Lord. **Call unto me and I will show thee great and mighty things, which thou knowest not.** This verse is from **Jeremiah 33:3** in the Bible. I was so overwhelmed when I received these words. God is so good, He is so faithful. When the Lord sees our anxious hearts wanting to follow Him more diligently and loving Him even more, He in return will touch our hearts with wonderful words of love. We have the assurance that when we call unto Him He will definitely answer us and show us great and mighty things. God's love has no limits.

13th September 2009—I was watching Israel Night on God TV, and an Iranian person was testifying of how he came to believe in the Lord Jesus Christ. His testimony really encouraged me as I followed the programme and gave it my undivided attention. Early the next morning

I woke up seeing a beautiful dream. In this dream I was in my living room and I saw the open sky covered with glittering stars, they were gold and studded with beautiful coloured precious stones, the stars were uncountable. When I saw the stars, I said, "So this is what the word of God says, 'They shall shine like the stars in the sky'." **Daniel 12:3.** I believe when we receive good things into our spirit we reap good things, "What we sow we reap". The Word of God is pure and unadulterated; when we ask the Holy Spirit to guard our hearts, He will lead and guide us to read His Word, listen to good Christian messages and songs, read good books, watch Christian TV etc. He is the One who can bless each and every one of us with all these privileges. We need to pray and ask the Holy Spirit to prepare us for the coming of the Lord. The Bride of Christ has to be pure and spotless. We should listen to the voice of the Holy Spirit speaking to us; He will help us, when we seek the Lord with all our hearts.

20ᵗʰ September 2009—This morning I woke up singing Hallelujah songs with a group of Christians and there were many non-believers listening. The Hallelujahs we sang were beautiful tunes which I had never heard before, but we all knew how to sing them, and I asked a girl who was watching us sing, to sing as well, and she too joined us in the singing. We should all sing Hallelujah all the time, that's what we will be singing in heaven, and basking in the presence and love of God.

10ᵗʰ October 2009—Early in the morning in a dream the Lord showed me a big book with a light blue cover and clean white pages. It was in a cellophane cover, the cellophane paper was uncovered and I received the clean book. I asked the Lord for the meaning, I felt that this could be my next upgraded book. This was just as I had finished writing my book "The Light of the Harvest".

26ᵗʰ February 2010—I had a dream that I was eating a fruit with a small group of people, we then held hands in a circle and the circle became larger and larger and I saw a very large circle of people, all were holding hands and singing and praying together. There was plenty of light, which I believe was the presence of the Lord. This relates to the "Light of the Harvest" book that my friends and I started distributing together lately. I believe as we use these books as an evangelism tool to witness to others with the message of the love of God, He in return will encourage us to go even further in the work He has entrusted to us. The Lord is mindful of every little job we do for his glory on a daily basis.

25ᵗʰ April 2010—I started distributing my very first magazine of the "Light of the Harvest" to many people as I wanted to spread the Good News. Then the Lord gave me these encouraging words, **"Multimedia will be targeted and you will be anointed and used".** The Lord loves to see us proclaim His word in many ways to the multimedia. I thank the Lord for His concern on the work we do for His glory.

26ᵗʰ June 2010—I woke up this morning singing a song **"The Spirit of the Lord has come, has come, has come, The Spirit of the Lord has come, has come, has come".** There were many people getting ready to clap and sing this song. I believe in these last days many are being filled with His Holy Spirit. Prayer is a two-way conversation with the Lord. I pray daily and claim the promise below. I believe the Lord gave me this beautiful song in answer to my prayer. **Acts 2:17-18** "And it shall come to pass in the last days, saith God, I will pour out my Spirit upon all flesh; and your sons and your daughters shall prophesy, and your young men shall see visions, and your old men shall dream dreams; and on my servants and on my handmaids I will pour out in those days of my Spirit, and they shall prophesy."

15th July 2010—When we pray the Lord does speak to us in dreams, visions and various ways that our prayers are answered. It is the Holy Spirit that leads and guides us to pray as we keep listening to His voice. I pray every day for England and the British Isles and the nations all over the world as the Spirit leads. In a dream I saw the whole map of England which was fully blue in colour and only a small fraction on one side of the map was red. Blue spiritually means heavenly. I believe there will be a great revival in England. Praise God for the believers who pray continually for revival, that the Lord will pour out His Holy Spirit upon all flesh over England and the whole of the British Isles, so that people will repent and turn to God with one accord. The prayers of the saints will never go unanswered. If we ask the Father anything in the name of Jesus according to His will He will hear us.

17th July 2010—This morning before I woke up, I saw a beautiful radio placed on a table and a beautiful song was sung, **"The King is coming!"**. It was a heavenly tune with many languages including the Hebrew language. There were many types of food for the preparation of the Banquet. I also heard the word "The gold cup for you". I believe the Lord is preparing the Bride of Christ and we will receive gold cups at His banqueting table. The Holy Spirit is preparing pure and spotless brides for the soon coming Bridegroom Jesus Christ our Lord and Saviour.

4th August 2010—After a time of prayer in the early hours of the morning I was woken up a couple of hours later, when I saw a vision that I was in a moonlit garden. A beautiful pure white dove came flying towards me twice like a mighty rushing wind. I also saw two people dressed in pure long white garments in that place. It was like heaven, I had never seen such a beautiful powerful dove like that before. The vision was very vivid. I felt the awesome presence of the Holy Spirit, it was joy unexplainable.

19th October 2010—Whenever the Lord wakes me up in the night I take the opportunity to pray and then go back to sleep; to my amazement I was woken up, and in a vision I saw a beautiful white bouquet of flowers, very natural, the flowers were opening up, with life in them. They were extremely beautiful large white roses. I know for sure I will see these beautiful flowers in heaven. Very often when I speak to the Lord, I always say that my one desire is to walk with the Lord in the beautiful heavenly garden of flowers. I believe He revealed himself to me in this way in answer to my prayer.

24th October 2010—I had a vision last night that I was in a very bright place. I saw something like a large flower that was lit up with silver lines. It started moving and opening up; to my surprise, I then saw a tall person in white robes walking towards the place and this large flower was moving and opening up magnificently. As I was watching, I noticed that the petals were all angels—they were moving around in a dance in glittering white and silver garments. What a wonderful sight it was, the Lord has many surprises for us when we all get to heaven. We read in **I Corinthians 2:9** "Eye hath not seen, nor ear heard, neither have entered into the heart of man, the things which God hath prepared for them that love him."

2nd December 2010—I had a dream that my bed had a beautiful gold coverlet with gold flowers embroidered on it. I was amazed to see this beautiful bedspread on my bed. I believe the Lord reminded me about our works which will be tested with fire. I presume that my prayer time was tested with fire and came through as gold. For over six months whenever the Lord woke me up, instead of reading the Bible as I had been doing usually, I felt led to get off my bed and spend an hour in prayer with the Lord. Although it was not easy, by the help of the Holy Spirit, I have been continuing to pray in the nights and I believe the Lord has welcomed my prayer time at the break of dawn.

4th December 2010—This morning before I woke up, in a dream I saw the palm of my right hand and all my fingers were covered with oil. I presume as believers in Christ, the oil represents the anointing of the Holy Spirit, and the Lord has given us the power to lay on hands and pray for one another; I have been doing this whenever I was led by the Holy Spirit on many occasions, either by holding hands together and praying for one another or in groups with other believers. We see in the Bible in **Mark**

16:17 "And these signs shall follow those who believe: In my name shall they cast out demons; they shall speak with new tongues; They shall take up serpents; and if they drink any deadly thing, it shall not hurt them; they shall lay hands on the sick and they shall recover." When we exercise our faith and lay hands on the sick in obedience to His word, the Lord will heal the sick as He has promised. God is not a respecter of persons.

20th December 2010—God is concerned in little things. Last night I dreamt that our front garden which had been covered with snow, was now clear, and the grass was green, and the sun was shining. This was because I was anxious about attending Church on Christmas Day. The Lord was very gracious to reveal to me by this dream that on Christmas Day the sun will be shining and the grass will be green so that I don't have to worry about it. I was glad on Christmas Day my dream came to pass, as the snow had melted and the grass was green and there was a little sunshine as well which enabled me to get to Church without any worry. What amazing love God has for us, even in little things that we are anxious about, He will make sure to bless us.

****

GLIMPSES OF HEAVEN

Psalm 37:4 "Delight thyself also in the Lord, and he shall give thee the desires of thine heart. Commit thy way unto the Lord, trust also in him, and he shall bring it to pass." Our Heavenly Father has given us many promises from His precious Word. He has a unique plan for each and every one of us. God has chosen us before the foundation of the world. His love is immeasurable; His one desire is to accomplish all His plans and purposes in our lives. When we take delight in Him and commit all our dreams and plans into His hands, He will bring it to pass. It is the Lord who directs our paths. God is faithful to His word and He will give us the deep secret desires of our hearts. The more we stand on God's promises and trust in Him, confess His word, believing what He says is true, He is able to accomplish what He has promised.

God's heart of love is unconditional, He wants to bless us with many surprises. According to Psalm139, God's thoughts towards us are countless as the sand on the seashore. Jesus' sacrificial death on the cross of Calvary, and His shed blood for us, made it possible for man to be restored back to Him. Jesus sent us the Comforter, the Holy Spirit, to lead and guide us into all truth. He will convict us of sin and bring us to a place of true repentance. God wants to fill us with His Holy Spirit and reveal His glory to all believers who belong to the Church, the Body of Christ. **Acts: 2:17-18** "And it shall come to pass in the last days, saith God, I will pour out of my Spirit upon all flesh; and your sons and your daughters shall prophesy, and your young men shall see visions and your old men shall dream dreams; and on my servants and on my handmaidens I will pour out in those days of my Spirit, and they shall prophesy."

Every night I pray and ask the Lord for a glimpse of heaven. God is faithful, He has revealed many secrets of His heavenly kingdom. God is not a respecter of persons, He loves to give good gifts to all His children. The Lord wants us to love Him with all our heart, all our soul, all our mind and all our strength, He is faithful to bless us with many spiritual blessings. There was a time in my walk with God, when I started reading the book the "Father's love letter" and was speaking to the Father all the time, then the Holy Spirit revealed to me in a powerful way that **Jesus is the Author and the Finisher of our faith**. The Father has given all authority in heaven and on earth to His Son Jesus Christ. I soon realised that when we press on to have an intimate relationship with Jesus, our Saviour, He is faithful to reveal more of His heavenly kingdom.

When the Lord reveals glimpses of heaven to me, I pray and ask for the interpretation of what He has shown me by His Spirit.

One night I was singing praises to the Lord on my bed for a very long time before I fell asleep, and to my amazement I saw another vision of the Holy Spirit coming down towards me in the form of a dove for the second time, like a mighty rushing wind in a vision, about three times, it was very vivid and I knew I was fully awake to see this wonderful awesome presence and power of the Holy Spirit all over me. This was unspeakable joy to experience once again. The more we speak to the Lord and ask Him to reveal heavenly visions and glimpses of heaven, He is faithful to reveal this beautiful place called heaven where He is preparing mansions for His children as He has promised in His Word. Jesus said, "In my Father's house there are many mansions, and I go to prepare a place for you". What a blessed hope this is for all believers in Christ. This makes me more conscious of taking time to listen to His voice speaking to me. Some dreams are easy to understand but some are not, however through prayer we can be assured that He surely will reveal His secrets to His servants the prophets. We read in

I Corinthians 13:12 "For now we see through a glass darkly; but then face to face; now I know in part, but then shall I know even as also I am known."

The People are the Harvest

Ephesians 1:3-7 "Blessed be the God and Father of our Lord Jesus Christ, who hath blessed us with all spiritual blessings in heavenly places in Christ: According as he hath chosen us in him before the foundation of the world, that we should be holy and without blame before him in love: Having predestined us unto the adoption of children by Jesus Christ to himself, according to the good pleasure of his will, To the praise of the glory of his grace, wherein he hath made us accepted in the beloved. In whom we have redemption through his blood, the forgiveness of sins, according to the riches of his grace;"

TESTIMONY
A Friend in Need—*By Antonita*

I came to know Angela Goonewardene in 1980 at the Salvation Army Young Women's hostel. Originally I was a Roman Catholic. Angela led me to Christ. She was working at the International Correspondence Institute, a ministry of the Assemblies of God, and she introduced us to the Bible Correspondence courses, which my friends and I were interested in and gladly followed. Then she invited me to church and as I had accepted the Lord as my personal Saviour, I was baptised at the Assembly of God Church in Colombo in 1981.

A couple of years later I came to England. After some time I met Angela when she came to Cheshire, England. A few years later when she came to London she stayed with me for three years. During this period we prayed together and I learned to pray.

In 1998 I was diagnosed with breast cancer. Angela gave me great support and prayed for me earnestly. God answered all the prayers, and miraculously I was healed. I thank and praise God for giving me a new life. Even after moving from my place, whenever I have difficulties and problems I telephone Angela and she prays with me without any hesitation. She is a prayer warrior and she is my prayer partner, we pray for each other. In January 2009 I fell asleep in the bus returning from work. The bus driver (maybe a message from the Lord) took me to hospital and I was diagnosed with meningitis. I called Angela from the hospital and she prayed for me. God saved my life again. He gave me a new lease of life. May God bless her ministry. I thank God for this faithful friend He has given me.

Antonita Sebamalai, London.

TESTIMONY
By Janet

I have known Angela Goonewardene since the year 2000 when I first attended the Elim Pentecostal Church in Clapham, a very live church devoted to God and His glory, and to the Kingdom of God.

Angela and I did not know each other well until 2004, when she invited me to the New Christians Fellowship at the church. As Administrator, she is very caring about the whole body of the church. Every member matters to her, whether they attend the church or not.

Over the years, she has become a very dear friend, and even now, when I have moved on to another church, she remains an inspiration to me.

Her love and trust in our Lord is total, she is utterly devoted to God, Father, Son and Holy Spirit. She invited me because something, I believe it was the Lord, told her to, because I was lonely. I had never told her this.

She has great honour and integrity. She has taught me to pray more, to love God more. Teacher, little mother, guide. I pray this book will touch the hearts of all who read it. My life is richer with Angela in it. I thank God for her. May all glory be to God.

Janet Sinclair, London.

TESTIMONY
By Kathy

It is with great joy that I share this with you—it is such an awesome thing to be saved by the blood of the Lord Jesus and to know that your name is written in the Lamb's book of life, and that you will live for eternity in the presence of Jesus Christ your Lord and Saviour.

All this was possible for me because of the patient and persistent witnessing by the late Rev. Emmanuel Bosco Goonewardene, who is Angela's beloved brother . . . . who was at that time an Evangelist. He never ever gave up witnessing to my father who was a tough man—a Naval Officer—it wasn't easy . . . it was hard work . . . lots of challenging questions to answer, lengthy discussions and debates etc; but Bro Bosco never gave up; he was faithfully there at every available opportunity to witness God's love, grace and mercy to my father.

Finally, when my father made the decision to accept the Lord Jesus as his personal Saviour, there was no turning back and everything changed in our home and so all of us his children were led to the Lord. It was like magic—which meant no more reciting prayers from a prayer book and confessing your sins to a man (priest), instead you simply talked to Jesus directly, pouring your heart out to Him. The blessed assurance that He loves you with an unconditional love, and is always by your side, He never will leave you and He is a friend that is closer than a brother.

It is so comforting to feel and sense His presence with you when you are afraid and alone. It's just unexplainable; you have got to experience it yourself. Trusting the Lord totally with child-like faith is the best thing you should do, and watch Jesus do the rest. Yes, I was a Roman Catholic and came to know Jesus in 1974; since then my life has changed and He has seen me through the highs and the lows . . . even when I went through the valley of disappointment and despair the Lord was always with me and helped me through my pain. He turned my mourning into dancing for me and blessed me abundantly. I love my Lord with all my heart and soul.

In closing I would like to say, to God the only God who saves us through Jesus Christ our Lord, be glory and majesty, dominion and power before all time and now and forever, Amen. (Jude 25).

God Bless

Kathy Tharumanayagam
England

TESTIMONY
By Maria

Angela Goonewardene is a beloved daughter of God. She has with her insightful book and her friendship been able to share with me the love that God has for his children here on earth. I feel blessed to be able to count Angela as my friend. Her patience and her unquestioning support have helped me in my life, especially through some hard challenges that I have faced in the last year or so. May she continue with God's work, and may He continue to use her to bring people to Him. Angela, may God bless you all the days of your life.

Maria Oladapo,
London

****

To God be the glory, great things He has done!

MESSAGES GIVEN TO ME BY THE LORD FIRST TO PRINT AND THEN TO UPGRADE THE BOOK

15th November 2005—In a vision this morning, I saw that someone handed a book to me from above. A page was open. The first page had the face of Jesus on it. The second page, facing that, had pictures of children and families and other people. The words "**Light of the Harvest**" were on the book that I saw, the name given to me to print the book. I believe Jesus is the Light, the People are the Harvest. There were more pages in the book. I had no clue at that time regarding printing a booklet.

9th January 2006—I saw another page of the **Light of the Harvest** starting with **Jesus and me.** I felt it was time to start writing the book and I wrote my personal testimony.

8th February 2006—Before I woke up this morning I saw in a dream that the **Light of the Harvest** magazine was completed. A reminder to start printing the magazine.

23rd March 2006—Early this morning I woke up and was reading the Gospel of Mark, and the Lord was speaking to me by His Spirit with clear words: **Write the Vision on Tables**. I looked at what I was reading which was the book of Mark, but the words **Write the Vision on Tables**

came from deep within. Another urgent confirmation that I write the vision and make it plain on tables. This is relating to the **Light of the Harvest** magazine He wants me to complete.

8th October 2007—Do another re-print. Words I received very early this morning. This relates to the Light of the Harvest Magazine which I have completed and given for printing. Once again I believe the Lord wants me to do another print.

****

In obedience to the Lord I have completed another *upgraded version* of the "Light of the Harvest" book. I praise God for the leading and guiding of the Holy Spirit in enabling me to establish what He wants me to establish relating to His marvellous work in my life.

Pray for the peace of Jerusalem;
they shall prosper that love thee.
Psalm 122:6

And the Spirit and the bride say, Come.
And let him that heareth say, Come.
And let him that is athirst Come!
And whosoever will, let him take the water of life freely.
Revelation 22:17

Surely, I come quickly. Amen.
Even so, come Lord Jesus.
Revelation 22:20b

Revised Version—2014

Part 1

Light of the Harvest

Recent Amazing Vision of Jesus Awesome in All His
Glory, Splendour and Majesty
A Joyous Day of My Life!

Recent Amazing Vision of 'Jesus and Me'—May 6th 2013 at 3.00 p.m.

At 3.00 p.m. this afternoon as I was resting at the feet of Jesus on my sofa, first I saw Jesus walking in the garden and I said I want to see His golden **girdle** (girdle, sash or band). Within a few minutes Jesus revealed to me first a burning branch tested with fire, and then Jesus himself in a beautiful garment covered with a beautiful design of gold and silver, awesome in majesty. A light bright as the sun shone on my right shoulder, then I felt warm on that side, then I was changed into a beautiful white garment and I was laying on Jesus' breast. Then the phone rang four times, but I did not answer, however, when the scene was changing I got up and saw that my friend June Ryde had called me four times and when I tried to get her on line there was no response.

I was very sad that I had got up, and again I went back to lay my head down at Jesus' feet. Then I saw the burning branch again, and Jesus appeared majestically walking towards me and stepped in once again. This time two bright lights shone on my right and left shoulders. Again I saw Jesus standing in soft white raiment of gold and silver, with a beautiful design all over his garment, awesome, full of majesty, and I saw myself as a bride in pure white soft bridal garments wearing a long white veil with a golden bouquet of flowers walking towards Jesus gracefully. This is such an amazing miracle as I knew what I was seeing very vividly was myself as His bride of Christ.

As I had high blood pressure, I had sent emails to some of my close friends requesting them to pray for good results, then I saw June's message on my emails. This was her reply. Dear Angela, you are in my prayers! I see you completely healed by GRACE. Love and hugs, June.

A result of the message from June Ryde on the telephone when I was laying my head on Jesus' breast has been a message from the Lord that I have been healed. Now I know that as most of my friends have prayed for me, this prayer has been answered and I have been healed by His GRACE. I praise His wonderful name!

The True Vine: The Holy Spirit gave the interpretation of the burning branch in the garden. Read **John 15:1-2 "I AM the true vine, and my Father is the husbandman. Every branch in me that beareth not fruit he taketh away: and every branch that beareth fruit, he purgeth it, that it may bring forth more fruit."**

The golden bouquet: Tested with fire and come through as gold.

2 Corinthians 5:21 "For he hath made him to be sin for us, who knew no sin; that we might be made the righteousness of God in him."

Thoughts: AFTER THE FIRST VISION:

I was thinking of the golden bouquet the Lord had given me and wondered if they were roses, as I saw myself walking gracefully towards Jesus with a golden bouquet in my hand. And what about my two sisters, as I have been praying for them every day.

Jesus appears again for the second time today:

This time, I was having my tea and watching the "700 Hundred Club News" on "Revelation TV" then I happened to close my eyes, and again I saw the Vision of Jesus and me. Jesus showed me my golden bouquet of flowers, they were large roses, enlarged in size, and I saw it very vividly. Then I saw my two sisters and I all beautifully dressed as brides in white garments walking towards Jesus, they had golden bouquets as well, I was so amazed and happy to see the three of us together with Jesus as I had prayed for them every day without fail.

Long before this vision I had seen my sisters, in dreams, separately dressed in gold and white and one of them had a golden bouquet of flowers. Today I saw all three of us as brides ready for the Bridegroom – Jesus our Saviour and Lord—The Soon Coming King of kings and Lord of lords. Today's vision is the most awesome vision I had ever seen in one day at two different times. Between 3.00 p.m. and 6.30 p.m. Jesus the most beautiful Bridegroom ever to see so vividly. Awesome God! And He shall be called Wonderful Counsellor, Mighty God, Everlasting Father, and Prince of Peace! Get excited! Jesus is coming soon!!!

God is good! All the time! His Precious Blood has washed us clean and made us whole. Praise God! **Romans 8:1a "There is therefore now no condemnation to them which are in Christ Jesus,"**

* * *

Highlights of Recent Amazing Visions of 'Jesus and me' Continues . . .

Jesus is Beautiful, Awesome and Adorable.
6th May 2013
Jesus appears again. I was in bed watching the God Channel and praying in tongues when suddenly I saw a vision of beautiful green leaves blowing in the wind. I walked through the branches and noticed that my veil was covered with white flowers at the back of my head while Jesus, my Saviour the loveliest one, was standing on the other side waiting for me. He looked at me and I bowed down and worshipped Him, then Jesus held me very close to Him.

7th May 2013
This morning during my prayer time, I had Communion and as I was worshipping the Lord, I saw a vision of my table with a vase and a burning bush on it, also there was a goldish colour tall communion cup on my table. This was amazing because I did not see anything else on my table, other than what I saw in the vision. I had learned to take communion on a daily basis from two of my close friends who do the same, and within a month I saw this vision. The Lord is very concerned with what we do, with regard to His Word.

1 Corinthians 11: 26. "For as often as ye eat this bread, and drink this cup, ye do shew the Lord's death till he come."

Acts 2:42 "And they continued steadfastly in the apostles' doctrine and fellowship, and in breaking of bread, and in prayers."

7th May 2013

At 'Prayer Soaking' at the Elim Pentecostal Church, Margaret was taking the service and as she laid hands on me and prayed for me, suddenly I was seeing a vision of the front of the Church. There were burning bushes in the front of the Church and I saw many Gold Shields and other Gold Trophies and a grand Organ and Piano were there, in the Church. This was really awesome. I was reminded, after I saw the vision, of the dedicated work of the Lord, in the Choir and many other ministries of the Church.

12th May 2013

During the Sunday morning service at Church while the Choir and believers were singing and worshipping the Lord, I was seeing beautiful visions of the heavenly places, with green trees, and the wind of the Holy Spirit was moving in this open space, it looked like a large garden and to my amazement, suddenly I saw an awesome white dove flying across the sky. As we were singing, flowers were opening and closing to the music. Heaven is a marvellous place to be with Jesus for ever. The Lord inhabits the praises of His people. The Lord delights to see His people worship and praise the Lord together in His Sanctuary. Every day the Lord was revealing many beautiful places in heaven, which were new to me and awesome to see these wonderful heavenly sceneries as He prepares us, the Bride of Christ, to be with the Lord, for ever and ever some day very soon.

13th May 2013—Communion with Jesus
During my prayer time this morning and taking Communion, Jesus lovingly was holding me close to Him. Every time I see the Lord, I see myself wearing a beautiful bridal dress which the Lord has given me. Today, the Lord showed me the ornaments of a big "Rose" on the sleeves of my bridal dress. This same night, in a vision Jesus himself put a face veil on me.

14th May 2013
This morning in a dream I woke up singing "Joy to the World, the Lord is come" with two other children. This evening as I was getting ready to sleep, I was seeing a vision of the Lord and me, in a wide open space with many trees and there was a wind blowing heavily that we had to hold our veils down. Jesus was holding me close to Him and I felt the beautiful presence of the Holy Spirit in that place. Jesus is real and heaven is real, there is no other place one would like to be, other than in this beautiful place called heaven.

15th May 2013
Jesus reveals the beautiful ornaments and flowers on my head and veil at the back of the head. They are gold and shiny precious stones.

16th May 2013
Revelation 21: 2-3 "And I John saw the holy city, new Jerusalem, coming down from God out of heaven, prepared as a bride adorned for her husband. And I heard a great voice out of heaven saying, Behold, the tabernacle of God is with men, and he will dwell with them, and they shall be his people, and God himself shall be with them, and be their God."

The Lord in a vision revealed to me the beautiful city of Jerusalem, it was late in the evening with lights shining all over the city, and then I saw all the lights coming together and forming in the image of Christ Jesus, ready to come down from heaven. This was an awesome vision of Jesus.

In another vision Jesus was teaching all His Brides to dance with Him. We first came down from the heavenly golden stairs, and then we were taught to dance gracefully holding hands in rows and then in a circle and to dance in beautiful displays to the music.

Jesus shows me in visions that He is always with me. I saw myself very vividly with my beautiful white veil and face veil, enlarged and shown to me. I felt a powerful light shine all over me, and the Holy Spirit revealing himself with the wind of the Spirit. Many times I see Jesus holding me close to Him, with His arms around me. I see in visions Jesus, and many brides of Christ, clapping and dancing in His banqueting hall, with long tables laid, ready for the "Marriage supper of the Lamb". This is very exciting! Heaven is an awesome, beautiful, wonderful, happy, enjoyable place to look forward to, to be with the "Saviour of the world" who has redeemed us with His precious blood and given us a free gift by faith in Christ Jesus, to live with Him for ever and ever.

18th May 2013
Jesus appeared again in a flash. Jesus was wearing a silky pure white garment. The top of it was full of precious stones, of many colours of gold, blue, red, they looked diamond shaped. This was an amazing vision to see in a flash. **Jesus is beautiful, awesome and adorable.**

19th May 2013
Jesus and me – At Sunday service, at our church this morning, Jesus was with me, and I was closely standing with His arms around me. I then saw on the projector in the church, although my eyes were closed, the cross and the words of the song we were singing "O Christ of burning cleansing flame – send the fire today". At the closing of the service I saw many brides in our church in pure white bridal garments walking towards Jesus in the vision at our Church.

20th May 2013
Today I saw Jesus and me in a vision enlarged in our bridal garments, they are beautiful pure white, with lace flowers at the top of the veil and Jesus probably in a "prayer shawl" – gold and white, His garments are silky and gold, with beautiful embroidery and flowing at the borders. We the brides were at His banqueting table, and then we all learned to clap and hold hands in a dance at times, and in beautiful dance displays, before the Lord. Our clothes are as light as we form ourselves as flowers in a display before Him, and bow down in worship; it

is an awesome dance before the Lord – unexplainable. **"When he shall appear, we shall be like him; for we shall see him as he is." 1 John 3:2b.**

21ˢᵗ May 2013
Today, I was seeing many visions of Jesus as usual. The rose on my hair, enlarged on my veil, is like white organdie and gold. In the church I was with the rest at "prayer soaking" waving a flag to Jesus and singing "How Great Is our God" as Margaret was leading the meeting. I saw myself with Jesus for a very long time, and then I saw a few who were at prayer soaking were gathering in a circle and holding hands. This is what the Lord had shown me many times to "agree and pray together."

This evening at around 7.00 p.m. I was seeing "Jesus and me" in enlarged pictures in our bridal garments, the lace in the borders of our garments and the beautiful work of embroidery on Jesus' prayer shawl is awesome! God's marvellous work in embroidery. Praise God!

25ᵗʰ May 2013
Praying in tongues: The whole day I was praying in tongues and I was seeing "Jesus and me" throughout the day. Sometimes I see Jesus and me in enlarged pictures dressed in wedding garments, pure white, beautifully designed with flowers and veils and even the face veil; our garments are pure white and very light. My eyes are glowing and covered with eye-sap, as I see Jesus' eyes they are beautiful and shining. Jesus is extremely adorable, awesome to look at, such beautiful eyes.

26th May 2013

Glory Zone: Early this morning I was woken up with the words "Glory Zone" and I started speaking in tongues, then Jesus came to me, and led me to a place of worship. He put on me a beautiful prayer shawl with many colours, like precious stones as Jesus had many of them on Him. There were many intercessory prayer warriors and we were all praying and worshipping and I saw beautiful rain, like fire and sparkles of fireworks, was falling in that place; all of them were in white robes with prayer shawls interceding and praying. This was an awesome place of the glory of the Lord called the "Glory Zone".

27th May 2013

Communion with Jesus: Early this morning just before 4.00 a.m. in the morning my bed was shaking, as if an angel was waking me up, it was the same as yesterday, then Jesus brought a cup and gave me a sip of drink, it was like taking communion. I then had it, and continued praising God in tongues, before I went back to sleep.

28th May 2013

After that every day, early morning, I'm woken up and Jesus gives me a communion cup, and I drink it, and I see many others, all dressed as brides, given a sip of the cup that Jesus brings. Praise God for this wonderful fellowship we have with the Lord in heaven. This evening the Lord showed me that I was being blessed with beautiful shining gold ornaments and even a head-dress like a crown was placed on my head, as I was wearing my bridal garments and veil. Praise God! How Jesus loves us. This is real love, unconditional love to make us like Him.

29ᵗʰ May 2013

Today I saw myself as a perfect looking bride with everything fitted on my veil, with a gold head-dress. My veil is covered with flowers like roses. Jesus then gave me and all the brides a cup of His communion wine; we were all given a sip from it. Praise God! His work is perfect, all because of the Blood of Jesus and the finished work on the cross of Calvary; we have the privilege of taking communion with the Lord.

30ᵗʰ May 2013

Early this morning I was given a sip of Jesus' communion wine and all other brides received the same, then I was taken to a beautiful open heavenly place and as the floodgates were open, many saints gone before me came running towards me. I believe they are my loved ones and friends. Praise God, for Heaven is real and God's word is real and if we obey Him and follow the leading of the Holy Spirit, He will help us to become like Jesus, and His word says when He shall appear, we shall be like Him: for we will see Him as He is. **1 John 3:2b**

31ˢᵗ May 2013

I had Communion with Jesus early morning as I woke up to pray. Very soon we will meet Jesus in the air, as now I see all the tables ready for the "Wedding Supper of the Lamb" – Jesus and the Bride of Christ. I see ourselves dancing very gracefully with Jesus, as He teaches us to dance. Most of the Christian instrumentals and songs I play on C.D. during my prayer and worship time, I see Jesus teaching me, and the rest of the brides to dance. They are so beautiful and graceful. I praise God for the beautiful visions and dreams He shows me revealing His magnificent beauty and awesomeness. God is faithful! His never failing love and goodness and mercy will follow us all the days of our life, as we put our confidence and trust in Him. **Jesus is awesome, beautiful and adorable.**

*   *   *

Part 2

Light of the Harvest – 'Jesus and me' Amazing Visions—continued . . . .

But God, who is rich in mercy, for his great love wherewith he loved us, even when we were dead in sins, hath quickened us together with Christ, (by grace ye are saved;) and hath raised us up together, and made us sit together in heavenly places in Christ Jesus: Ephesians 2:4-6

What a loving Heavenly Father, who even when we were dead in sin and trespasses, has made us alive together to sit in the heavenly places with Christ Jesus. Although I knew this verse and have been always speaking it out, I had never experienced such awesome things as I now see in visions and dreams. Truly we are seated together with Christ in the heavenly places. Since the year 2012 I have been seeing Jesus almost every day, sometimes in vivid dreams and visions, but now starting from the 6th May 2013 when the Lord revealed to me the amazing vision of myself as a bride of Christ, and then seeing my two sisters and me walking towards Jesus as brides of Christ, was in reality like a dream come true. Something glorious to look forward to.

1 Corinthians 2:9
"But as it is written, Eye hath not seen, nor ear heard, neither have entered into the heart of man, the things which God hath prepared for them that love Him."

The more I spend time in His presence, the more Jesus reveals Himself to me. Some of the things I see cannot be explained—the beautiful bridal garments, the gold glittering crowns, face veils and long glittering strands on the veils and many multitudes of brides having been made ready for the `marriage supper of the Lamb` walking in long processions to a banqueting hall and then the worship and dancing begins, with Jesus in the midst of us. I see vast beautiful breathtaking places in heaven where Jesus takes us. The levels and levels of heights as we go up, and up to zones like glory zones. The brilliant colours of the rainbow and bright silver lights appearing in various ways are extraordinary and unexplainable. Sometimes I see our garments shining bright like the brightest clouds, white or silver or gold, the brightness is unexplainable.

1 Corinthians 13:12
"For now we see through a glass, darkly; but then face to face: now I know in part; but then shall I know even as also I am known."

Stage by stage the Lord was revealing the number of places He has used me to spread the Good News. I had a strong desire and willing heart and prayed every day that the Lord would use me and my talents for His glory. I believe in answer to prayer, I had many opportunities and doors were open. After seeing the recent vision on the 6th May 2013, I now see the Lord placing many beautiful ornaments and crowns and beautiful shawls, they are lavishly given to all His brides. I see the person dressed like a bride, putting all these beautiful ornaments on my veil and on my clothing. The Lord loves and adorns us extravagantly with His beauty, as written in the Bible.

1 John 3:2b. "When he shall appear, we shall be like him; for we shall see him as he is." Colossians 3:4. "When Christ, who is our life, shall appear, then shall ye also appear with him in glory."
According to the Bible there is no male or female, we are all like the angels in heaven, beautiful spirit beings in our glorious bodies. We are dressed as brides, as we are the Bride of Christ. God has blessed us with extravagant beautiful bridal garments, crowns and veils that cannot be described and bridal bouquets. We are joint-heirs with Jesus. What a blessed hope we have in Christ our Lord and Saviour Jesus Christ.

Romans 8:16-17 "The Spirit itself beareth witness with our spirit, that we are the children of God: and if children, then heirs; heirs of God, and joint-heirs with Christ; if so be that we suffer with him, that we may be also glorified together."

Prayer Changes Things:
In reality this is how the Lord can reveal Himself to us. Spending time with Him in prayer and supplication can bring many people, including our families and loved ones for whom we pray, down to their knees to accept Jesus Christ as their personal Saviour and Lord. Jesus said, "I am the Way, the Truth and the Life; no man comes to the Father but by Me". I'm thankful to the Lord for my late brother who led us to Christ. Today we have been set free as a result of prayer. I'm glad I can see the changes which have taken place in many of our family members and

loved ones who are believers in Christ and have been set free as we continued in prayer.

God's Agape Love – Jesus in dazzling gold

I can never forget the beautiful vision on the **3rd of September 2013** when the Lord woke me up at 4.00 a.m. I was seeing Jesus wearing a long garment of dazzling gold walking towards me and He held me close to Him, then I saw His loving arms enfolding me and comforting me feeling me on my shoulders and arms. I was so happy and blessed seeing Jesus so beautiful and lovingly caressing me, as I was so close to Him. What an awesome comforting and adorable Son of God, who is so concerned about me to love me in this way. I love my Jesus very much, as He draws me so close to Him. Jesus shows personal attention to His saints the bride of Christ. God's perfect love is manifested in His Son Jesus the Messiah.

God is not a Respecter of Persons. He loves each and every one of His brides, and pays individual attention to each person as they draw close to Him and love Him in return. We must always remember that He chose us, and gave us the gift of eternal life. Hallelujah! In reality this is Agape love God has for His children, manifested in Jesus Christ.

Jesus in His Beautiful Robes, Precious Stones and Colourful Prayer Shawls:

Revelation 21:3. Many times I have seen that Jesus and the awesome beautiful robe He wore had gold blocks of stone, with colourful stones, they looked like precious stones; I believe each stone represents us, the body of Christ.

Jesus the Bridegroom is adorned with the Body of Christ. **Revelation 21:3 "And I heard a great voice out of heaven saying, Behold, the tabernacle of God is with men, and he will dwell with them, and they shall be his people, and God himself shall be with them, and be their God."**

I saw the Lord in a long beautiful prayer shawl with the same colours of His Bridal garments in gold and precious stones of pink, emerald green and other colours. The pattern was different from the blocks of stones which I have seen before, they were smaller and cut stones. The brides were also wearing the same prayer shawls similar to what Jesus was wearing. They looked all alike and it was so amazing to see a vast number of these beautiful brides walking with Jesus very gracefully.

One morning I was woken up seeing Jesus in a vision in all His beauty, splendour and majesty clothed in gold and precious stones of many colours representing the body of Christ. What an awesome vision. Again in another vision, I saw many brides of Christ beautifully dressed in fine linen of white shiny bright robes, and they were all in a circle with their heads bowing down at the feet of Jesus. The floor was gold with precious stones where the brides were bowing down. The presence of the Lord was glorious and awesome!

I also saw these beautiful brides of Christ in a circle, around the colourful garments of Jesus who was standing in the midst of us. The brides had been forming a circle at the feet of Jesus. His garments are fitted with gold and precious stones of many colours. The Majesty and splendour of Jesus, the King of kings and the Lord of lords, is unexplainable.

Open Heaven a Reality

Early morning I woke up seeing a vision of an open heaven with many brides of Christ in a larger circle than I had seen a few days ago. I saw colourful precious stones on the Lord's garments and around this were the beautiful brides in a dance display, and in the middle of the circle, I saw a beautiful white dove going upwards higher and higher, reaching to the heavens above. This was wonderful to look at—words cannot express what I have seen these days. All the praise and glory goes to our Lord and Saviour Jesus Christ.

One afternoon while resting I was seeing Jesus in a vision. I noticed His eyes—they are beautiful and penetrating; lovely to look right into His eyes, and through the eyes I see beyond the image of Jesus and the glorious heavenly places. Sometimes I see Jesus looking right into my face, and all I see is His beautiful amazing eyes. I cannot stop thinking of my beautiful Saviour Jesus, His glory and splendour is extraordinary.

The Lord revealed to me a vision of Jesus in His magnificent garments of gold and colourful precious stones on his clothing. The brides of Jesus were all in fine linen, white long bridal garments and white long veils. In answer to prayer the Lord revealed to me that He covers His brides with the borders of His mantle over us. The power and the moving of the Holy Spirit were vivid and visible in this vision.

6th January 2014—Jesus the Light of the World

Early one morning I woke up seeing Jesus in a beautiful long white shiny robe, walking, and the sun was brightly shining behind Him as He walked. Jesus is the Light of the world. Jesus is our light as we walk in the Light of Him. Again I saw in another vision before I woke up one morning, I was with Jesus and I saw my glorious face with Him. This vision really amazed me.

This is an early morning vision when I saw the glorious image of Jesus, I wondered how awesome it is to see Jesus so beautiful – shining like the sun. The higher the Lord takes us with Him we look beautiful and shining. Jesus takes us from glory to glory into higher levels of His glory.

"When He shall appear we shall be like Him, for we shall see Him as He is."

Dancing with Jesus Gracefully

Early morning at 4.30 a.m. "Jesus and me" we were dancing. This was a beautiful vision—I couldn't open my eyes, because I wanted to see more of "Jesus and me" dancing so gracefully in our beautiful bridal garments. Jesus comes early morning and then I wake up to have fellowship with Him. Praise God! I see "Jesus and me" dancing together many times in visions and also the brides of Jesus dancing with us, but it was very significant as He started the day dancing with me. What a privilege to spend time with Jesus! What an awesome God we serve. He is full of love and compassion. Jesus is the most beautiful One I have ever seen and experienced in visions and dreams.

Extraordinary Colourful Prayer Shawls

I saw Jesus and all the brides were wearing prayer shawls of the same pattern full of coloured precious stones all over the prayer shawls. This was amazing and indescribable. I'm glad Jesus helps me wake up some mornings with a beautiful vision around 4.30 a.m.

In another vision Jesus woke me up around 4.30 a.m. He was wearing a beautiful robe of colours of precious stones on His garments and prayer shawl. It was like as if His garments were studded. The moving of the Holy Spirit was very powerful—when the garments were moving like a wind blowing over Jesus it was like a river flowing in that place. Very vivid vision – the awesome power of God – unexplainable.

Early morning at 4.00 a.m. I was woken up seeing a beautiful vision of Jesus seated and groups of brides were running towards Jesus. The place was fully lit up—it was an open heaven. Jesus was in brilliant white robes and all the brides were in shiny white robes, all in several groups running towards Jesus. The vision was so vivid to be able to remember a very bright heavenly place with Jesus seated. Jesus is awesome in beauty and majesty. Oh how I love my beautiful Jesus! He is so precious to me.

Awesome Mansions in Heaven

In an early morning vision the Lord woke me up and I was seeing a vision of beautiful houses like big mansions. I may have seen about six or seven mansions and each mansion was lit up with very bright lights. As I watched they were like lights shooting upwards from the back of each mansion. This was like the glory of God shining over each mansion. I then woke up as I knew the Lord wanted me to get up and pray. Jesus is the light of the world; there will be no sun in heaven as Jesus is the Light brighter than the sun and we will walk in the light of Jesus.

Before I woke up in the early hours of the morning I saw in a vision that I was walking with a few saints, brides of Christ; as we were walking a bright light shone, leading the way. I believe it was the light of Jesus. Jesus shines brighter than the sun.

This morning I woke up seeing a beautiful vision that I was covered with a shining colourful prayer shawl, it was studded with precious stones. Then I saw that we were all as brides of Christ in white apparel shining brightly in His glory and presence. What an awesome place heaven is and to be in the glorious home with Jesus forever and ever. Praise God!

*   *   *

Part 3

Light of the Harvest 'Jesus and me' Amazing Vision Continues . . . .

Jesus Robed in All His Glory Splendour and Majesty, the Most Admirable Bridegroom ever and His Beautiful Brides.

"But as it is written, Eye hath not seen, nor ear heard, neither have entered into the heart of man, the things which God hath prepared for them that love him. But God hath revealed them unto us by his Spirit: for the Spirit searcheth all things, yea, the deep things of God." 1Corinthians 2:9-10

Prayer—a two-way conversation with the Lord: I start my day with prayer asking the Holy Spirit to take full control over me and teach me to pray. It's the Holy Spirit that brings us close to Jesus. The Holy Spirit is the Third Person in the Blessed Trinity, Jesus sent us the Holy Spirit. He is called the Comforter, the Counsellor, the Spirit of God, Spirit of Truth, Spirit of Christ, Spirit of Wisdom, and the Helper who comes alongside to help us as we pray. The Holy Spirit gives us knowledge and understanding. He is just like Jesus. Praying in the Spirit and speaking in tongues is a direct communication with God. The Bride of Christ is fully dependent on the Holy Spirit to prepare us for the soon return of our Saviour and Lord Jesus Christ, to meet Him in the air. The Holy Spirit enables us to lift Jesus high as we sing and exalt the name of the Lord. He is always with us, leads and guides us, in our daily life and draws us more closer to God.

John 15:26 "But when the Comforter is come, whom I will send unto you from the Father, even the Spirit of truth, which proceedeth from the Father, he shall testify of me:"

The Reality of an Open Heaven: I know for sure, whenever I close my eyes and worship the Lord, I see myself in an open heaven. I see Jesus adorned in His amazing beautiful bridal robe of pure white with silk and embroidery interwoven in shiny sparkling gold, silver and precious stones holding me close to Him. I also see myself adorned in a beautiful white bridal robe filled with flowers of embroidery interwoven with shiny gold and silver on the robe and head-dress with extraordinary work on them. Jesus has lavished us with His extraordinary beauty and love despite our faults and failures. He thought of us when He sacrificed His life by shedding His precious blood for us and has given us eternal life. When He hung on that cross, Jesus said to the Father 'IT IS FINISHED'! What an awesome God we serve who has forgiven us of all our sins, past, present and future with one perfect sacrifice that Jesus paid for us on the cross of Calvary. Our perfect Heavenly Father has cast all our sins into the sea of forgetfulness never to remember them anymore. God's love is perfect, unconditional and everlasting. Hallelujah!

"For he hath made him to be sin for us, who knew no sin; that we might be made the righteousness of God in him." 2 Corinthians 5:21

"For if by one man's offence death reigned by one; much more they which receive abundance of grace and of the gift of righteousness shall reign in life by one, Jesus Christ." Romans 5:17

Profound Visions of Jesus in an Open Heaven

Praise God! I can enjoy my time of prayer on a daily basis. In reality the vision I saw on the 6th May 2013 continues. However, now I see Jesus in visions everyday as I pray. This is unexplainable, the amazing, unconditional love of Father God is expressed in our Lord and Saviour Jesus Christ who is the brightness of the Father's glory. I believe Jesus is the most admirable Bridegroom ever to see, clothed in His beautiful Bridal Robes of Righteousness. The border of His veil or prayer shawl that covers His head is pure white, with silk and embroidery. His face is covered with a light veil. His eyes are extremely beautiful, the loveliest eyes I have ever seen, they are bright, glowing, sparkling, penetrating and indescribable.

Whenever I see Jesus blink His eyes, I'm reminded that He is full of Life, as He is our life giver. His eyes are incredibly beautiful, awesome in wonder! Around His eyes, on his eyelids, I see a border of gold with glittering or shimmering precious stones, which cannot be explained, and through His eyes I can see beyond, the many beautiful heavenly places. All the brides of Christ look extra-ordinarily beautiful and they are all clothed in shining pure white robes of embroidery in soft raiment, these are the robes of righteousness. When He looks into my face, and talks with me, I see His lips moving and His teeth are sparkling, gold in colour, He is extremely beautiful, His smile is beyond comprehension. I'm glad we belong to an awesome wonderful Saviour who loves us immeasurably.

What a privilege to have an intimate, love relationship with Jesus. He is loving, kind, gracious and compassionate toward us. Jesus is always with us, He takes us, His brides, everywhere, to many far away heavenly places, and I see our robes shining like the brightest clouds of heaven. As I continue in prayer, sometimes, I see Jesus holding me close to Him, as we dance gracefully. These are the heights and levels the Lord takes us as we continue in His presence. I see many brides as we all gather in dance displays as we worship before our Lord and Saviour Jesus Christ. I believe the more we spend time in prayer and read His Holy Word, the Bible, the Lord delights in us, as He shows His extravagant love towards us, and takes us to higher levels of His glory. God's love is unconditional, immeasurable, with no limits. With the help of the Holy Spirit, my love for Jesus has incredibly grown. I love Jesus very much, and long for His soon return. Hallelujah!

Each day, as I spend time in prayer for the Peace of Jerusalem, for the Body of Christ, for family members and loved ones, for my Church and friends, for governments, and various other prayer needs, the Lord reveals to me the many people I have prayed for, and I see them clothed in robes of righteousness. They, too, join us in the heavenly places. I see vast places and myriads of Saints which cannot be numbered in worship before the Lord. I also see long rows of people almost everyday during my time of prayer, whom the Lord reveals to me, as He walks in Majesty along the aisle. He then meets me, and walks along with me as He shakes His hand with some of them, revealing to me the people for whom I have been praying, this is profound. I would have never known these amazing mysteries unless the Lord revealed them to me. The depth of His love is indescribable. What an awesome God we serve, I praise God for His goodness and mercy towards us, His children.

Even when I pray for the deaf to hear, the blind to see, the dumb to speak, the lame to walk, the lepers to be cleansed, the sick to be healed and many more, I see some of the people for whom I have prayed being healed. This reminds me of the great sacrifice the Lord has made through the precious Blood of Jesus and the complete, finished work on the Cross of Calvary that all these prayers have been answered.

Whenever I pray, and ask for more of the power of the Holy Spirit and more of Jesus, and more of His glory, the Lord takes me to higher heights, from glory to glory as I see the incredibly beautiful colours of the rainbow in the heavenly places, which is awesome in wonder!. The various and profound visions the Lord has revealed to me cannot be written down or even explained, in reality they are indescribable, mysteries that could never be understood, until I meet Jesus in heaven to be with Him forever and ever.

"For the Lord himself shall descend from heaven with a shout, with the voice of the archangel, and with the trump of God: and the dead in Christ shall rise first: then we which are alive and remain shall be caught up together with them in the clouds, to meet the Lord in the air: and so shall we ever be with

the Lord. Wherefore comfort one another with these words." I Thessalonians 4:16-18

"That if thou shalt confess with thy mouth the Lord Jesus, and shalt believe in thine heart that God hath raised him from the dead, thou shalt be saved." Romans 10:9

JESUS the most admirable Bridegroom is coming for a prepared Church as the Holy Spirit prepares the Bride of Christ for His soon return. Get excited!! He is coming soon to meet us in the air. What a wonderful day it is going to be when He comes to snatch His Bride away!

"But if the Spirit of him that raised up Jesus from the dead dwell in you, he that raised up Christ from the dead shall also quicken your mortal bodies by his Spirit that dwelleth in you." Romans 8:11

Below is the link of my E-book available online:

The Light of the Harvest – Amazing Visions a reality of Open Heaven

http://www.amazon.co.uk/LIGHT-OF-THE-HARVEST-ebook/dp/B009JU240G/ ref=cm_cr_pr_product_top#_

*   *   *

About the Author

Angela B. Goonewardene was Coordinator of the International Correspondence Institute (ICI) in Sri Lanka, prior to joining ICI Bible Study UK. Her evangelistic passion led her to be involved in ministry with Kensington Temple Church London, Hillsong Church London and Premier Christian Radio. At present, she is the Office Administrator at Elim Pentecostal Church, London.

Angela's deep passion and zeal for evangelism continue to drive her to reach out to many through personal evangelism. She effectively shares the Good News of Jesus Christ, His redeeming love and life-changing power, both in her life and ministry, with all those she meets on a daily basis. Personal Evangelism is as natural as breathing to her!

Lightning Source UK Ltd.
Milton Keynes UK
UKOW06f0922230815

257354UK00001BA/2/P